Performance-Based Curriculum for Social Studies

From Knowing to Showing

Helen L. Burz
Kit Marshall

Performance-Based Curriculum for Language Arts
Performance-Based Curriculum for Mathematics
Performance-Based Curriculum for Science
Performance-Based Curriculum for Social Studies

Performance-Based Curriculum for Social Studies

From Knowing to Showing

Helen L. Burz
Kit Marshall

CORWIN PRESS, INC.
A Sage Publications Company
Thousand Oaks, California

For information:

Corwin Press, Inc.
A Sage Publications Company
2455 Teller Road
Thousand Oaks, California 91320
E-mail: order@corwin.sagepub.com

SAGE Publications Ltd.
6 Bonhill Street
London EC2A 4PU
United Kingdom

SAGE Publications India Pvt. Ltd.
M-32 Market
Greater Kailash I
New Delhi 110 048 India

Printed in the United States of America

Library of Congress Cataloging-in-Publication Data

Burz, Helen L.
    Performance-based curriculum for social studies: From knowing to showing /
        Helen L. Burz, Kit Marshall.
        p.   cm. — (From knowing to showing)
    ISBN 0-8039-6500-1 (cloth : acid-free paper) — ISBN 0-8039-6501-X (pbk. : acid-free paper)
    1. Social sciences — Study and teaching — United States.   2. Curriculum planning —
    United States.   3. Competency-based education — United States.
    I. Marshall, Kit.   II. Title.   III. Series: Burz, Helen L.   From knowing to showing.
    LB1584.B838   1997
    300'.71'073 — dc21   97-45266

This book is printed on acid-free paper.

98 99 00 01 02 03 04   10 9 8 7 6 5 4 3 2 1

Production Editor: S. Marlene Head
Typesetting: Birmingham Letter & Graphic Services
Cover Designer: Marcia M. Rosenburg

TABLE OF CONTENTS

PREFACE

Traditionally, textbooks and curriculum guides have reflected a focus on content coverage. Districts, schools, and educational systems have looked to publishers to define, at least in general terms, *what* should be taught and the order in which it should be taught. The result has been to place an emphasis on what students need to *know*, often with little direction regarding the role of relevance and meaning for the learning.

The technological impact on society and a scan of future trends clearly delivers the message that just teaching information and "covering the book" is no longer a sufficient focus for instructional systems. Instead, instruction must go beyond the content taught and actively engage learners in demonstrating how they can select, interpret, use, and share selected information. Educators are quick to accept this shift but are faced with a real need for models that depict ways this might occur.

Performance-Based Curriculum for Social Studies provides a unique model for taking instruction from the traditional focus on content to a student-centered focus that aligns selected content with quality and context.

Because of the focus on content related to a particular content discipline, textbooks and curriculum frameworks and guides have had a strong influence on *how* content is taught. The result, often, has been to teach facts and basic functional skills in isolation of a meaningful, learner-centered approach. There has been no purpose in mind beyond having students know certain information and skills. These previous frameworks and guides have also separated curriculum from instruction and assessment. *Performance-Based Curriculum for Social Studies* offers a new organization and alignment of curriculum, instruction, and assessment around practical classroom application and does it in a way that readily allows teachers to use it.

Although not intended to be a complete daily curriculum guide, *Performance-Based Curriculum for Social Studies* provides a planning framework that includes numerous examples of performance-based social studies set in real-life contexts. The numerous performance benchmarks, at Grades 3, 5, 8, and 12, and strands can be used directly or as guides for customizing instruction toward relevant and meaningful application of important knowledge around critical social studies concepts. *Performance-Based Curriculum for Social Studies* can be used to guide the development of a social studies curriculum throughout a family of schools or by individual teachers within one classroom or by an instructional team.

The framework is divided into four major sections:
1. Introduction to *Performance-Based Curriculum for Social Studies*
2. The Content/Concept Standards for Social Studies
   and Performance Benchmarks for 3rd, 5th, 8th, and 12th Grades
3. Technology Connections
4. Performance Designers

The Introduction is organized around a friendly question-and-answer format. This section is central to the remainder of the framework and provides the rationale and organizational structure for the book. The introduction also contains a discussion of performance-based learning actions.

The Content/Concept Standards for Social Studies represent the best thinking of current national experts and provide the substance for each performance benchmark. These standards are organized by major strands within the discipline. Performance Benchmarks included in this section represent descriptions of what could be expected from a student who has a high degree of understanding of a content standard in a high-quality performance. For example, the student might be asked to solve a real-life problem or develop alternative solutions to an issue or question that requires a solid understanding of the content/concept standard at one of four developmental levels.

Technology Connections provide guidance for the application of technology in some manner to a performance benchmark. These strategies are appropriate for students who are accessing, producing, and disseminating information through technology.

The last section, Performance Designers, provides an analysis of the performance designer, which is a planning tool for teachers. It requires a focus on the key elements of content, competence, context, and quality criteria.

At the end of the book, design templates and reproducible masters (see Appendix: Blank Templates) provide practical tools that can be used to customize and create classroom instructional material that will empower teachers and students to be successful in "showing what they know."

ABOUT THE AUTHORS

HELEN L. BURZ

Helen L. Burz is a doctoral candidate at Oakland University in Rochester, Michigan, where she received her master of arts degree in teaching. She received her bachelor of science in education from Kent State University. Helen has taught at the preschool, elementary school, and college levels. She has also worked as a principal at the elementary and middle school levels. As an innovative leader in curriculum design and instructional delivery systems, she has led her schools to numerous state and national awards and recognition and was selected as Administrator of the Year in Michigan.

She has addressed integrated curriculum and interdisciplinary instruction for the Association for Supervision and Curriculum Development's (ASCD's) Professional Development Institute since 1985. Currently, she works as an educational consultant across North America, speaking and conducting training for future-focused, performance-based curriculum, instruction, and assessment.

KIT MARSHALL

Kit Marshall earned her Ph.D. at Stanford University in educational leadership in 1983 and her master's and BA at Sacramento State University in 1968. After teaching across all levels, developing state and national dissemination grants in innovative educational design, and site-level administration, she pursued further studies in organizational development and technology. She has received numerous awards for her work in restructuring curriculum, instruction, and assessment. Her book, *Teachers Helping Teachers*, published in 1985, was the first practical handbook for educators on team building and mentor teaching.

Currently living in California, Marshall is an international speaker and trainer in future-focused, performance-based curriculum, instruction, and assessment. She is CEO of Action Learning Systems, an educational restructuring company and President of The Learning Edge, a World Wide Web (WWW) site dedicated to networking restructuring schools and communities throughout North America

INTRODUCTION

Authentic *performance-based education* asks students to take their learning far beyond knowledge and basic skills. A *performance orientation* teaches students to be accountable for knowing what they are learning and why it is important and asks them to apply their knowledge in an observable and measurable *learning performance.*

This shift "from knowing to showing" means that everything we do—instruction, curriculum, assessment, evaluation, and reporting—will ultimately be focused on and organized around these learning performances.

Educators, parents, business and industry leaders, and community members throughout North America are coming to agree that students should be demonstrating what they are learning in observable and meaningful ways. However, we have all been to school. Generally, our collective experience of what school *is* has been very different from what we believe schools need to *become.* If we are to succeed in the difficult shift from content coverage to performance-based education, we will need to have new strategies for defining and organizing what we do around *significant learning performances.*

Performance-Based Curriculum for Social Studies has been developed to provide the tools and the structure for a logical, incremental transition to performance-based education. *Performance-Based Curriculum for Social Studies* is not intended to be a comprehensive curriculum; it is a curriculum framework. The various components of the framework provide structure and a focus that rigorously organizes *content* around *standards* and *performance* around *learning actions.*

IMPORTANT QUESTIONS AND ANSWERS ABOUT *PERFORMANCE-BASED CURRICULUM FOR SOCIAL STUDIES*

Content/Concept Standards

Where do the content/ concept standards come from for this framework?

This framework represents the best thinking of current national experts in the discipline of social studies. Although there is no official national standard for content areas, the National Council for the Social Studies has demonstrated strong national leadership and influence that could form the instructional focus in a K–12 social studies program. These recommendations have been used to form the content/concept foundation of this framework and are identified as content/concept standards.

How are the content/concept standards organized within this framework?

The discipline of social studies is organized by major strands within the discipline. These strands are listed and described in Chapter 1. They are power and instability, human migration, beliefs and organizations, human expressionism, and elements of social and political interaction.

How do I know which content/ concept standards to focus on with MY students?

What students should know by the end of four levels, specified as Grades 3, 5, 8, and 12, is described at the beginning of each content strand section in Chapter 1. These levels are identified to highlight the specific developmental stages the learner moves through in school. A 1st-grade teacher should teach to the development of the concepts identified at Grade 3. A 6th-grade teacher should use the 5th-grade and 8th-grade content/concepts to guide instruction. A 9th-grade or 10th-grade teacher should use the 8th-grade contents as a guide and teach to the 12th-grade content/concepts.

These identified standards provide the content/concept focus for the performance benchmarks within the discipline and within the four developmental levels. Each major strand is identified by a set of content/concepts standards and is followed by four performance benchmark pages: one at each of the four levels—3rd, 5th, 8th, and 12th grade.

Performance Benchmarks

What is a performance benchmark?

In *Performance-Based Curriculum for Social Studies*, a performance benchmark is a representative description of what could be expected from a student who has a high degree of understanding of a content standard and can use that content standard in a high-quality performance. For example, the student might be asked to solve a real-life problem or develop alternative solutions to an issue or question that requires a solid understanding of the content/concept standard. If the students don't have the knowledge, they will not do well in the benchmark.

Each performance benchmark is designed to target a particular developmental level identified as 3rd, 5th, 8th, and 12th grades. Many students will be able to perform at a higher level, and some will perform at a lower level at any given point. Where a student is in the benchmarking process will determine where he or she is in the continuous learning process so characteristic of performance-based education.

What are the components of a performance benchmark?

Each performance benchmark has

1. A **Key Organizing Question** that provides an initial focus for the performance benchmark and the content/concept standard addressed in the performance benchmark.

2. Performance-based **Key Competences (Learning Actions)** that specify what students need to do with what they know in the performance benchmark (refer to Figure 1.1, The Learning Actions Wheel, on page 6).

3. **Key Concepts and Content** from the discipline that define what students need to know in the performance benchmark.

4. **Two Performance Tasks,** or prompts, that provide the purpose, focus, and authenticity to the performance benchmarks. Having two tasks allows a teacher to ask for a group or individual performance, or even to ask for a repeat performance.

5. **Quality Criteria** or **"Look fors"** that precisely describe what a student would do to perform at a high-quality level on that performance benchmark. This component serves as the focus for the evaluation process. How well students can demonstrate what is described in the quality criteria informs the evaluator about continuous improvement planning goals for a student. The profile that results from an entire classroom's performance benchmark informs the teacher regarding next steps in the teaching-learning process.

How do I use the performance benchmarks to inform and guide ongoing instruction and assessment?

The performance benchmarks will

-   Organize *what* you teach around a clear set of content/concept standards for a particular discipline

-   Organize *how* you teach by focusing your planning on the learning actions that you will teach and assess directly during daily instruction

-   Provide you with specific targets for your instruction—you will teach "toward" the performance benchmarks

-   Focus your students on what they will need to demonstrate in a formal evaluation of their learning

-   Communicate to parents that there is a clear and rigorous academic focus to authentic performance-based education

The performance benchmarks are primarily for evaluation of learning, *after* the learning has occurred. The performance designer, on the other hand, provides the focus for quality continuous improvement *during* the ongoing daily instructional process.

Technology Connections

How about a technology connection for Performance-Based Curriculum for Social Studies?

A number of performance benchmarks in *Performance-Based Curriculum for Social Studies* have a companion application that uses technology in some portion of the performance. If students are currently accessing, producing, and disseminating using technology, you will want to use or expand the strategies found in this section. These technology connections also serve as examples for teachers who are just moving toward the use of technology in their classrooms.

**Computer
Icon**

If there is a computer icon on the performance benchmark page, you can refer to the companion page that will extend the performance benchmark to involve technology.

Performance Designers

**What is a performance
designer?**

A performance designer is an organizer that is used to plan for ongoing performance-based instruction and assessment. The performance designer in *Performance-Based Curriculum for Social Studies* uses the learning actions and connects them to content, context, and criteria. The power of these learning actions becomes apparent when students begin to recognize and improve their competence with each new learning performance.

**How is the performance
designer used?**

The performance designer can be used to organize student performances in any discipline and with students at all developmental levels and in all grades.

The sample performance designers provided can be used just as they are or can serve as a starting point for new designs.

You are invited to copy the blank performance designers in the Appendix for your own classroom use, or you may want to create a new performance designer that fits your style of planning and thinking.

**How can I design
performances for
my students?**

Performances can be designed by following the steps provided in Chapter 3 on performance designers.

PERFORMANCE-BASED LEARNING ACTIONS

Learning actions organize what the students will *do* with what they *know* in each performance benchmark. Performance-based learning actions are based on four important beliefs:

1. *Learning is a quality continuous improvement process.*	Students improve their performance with any learning when they have multiple opportunities to apply what they know in a variety of settings over time. As students become familiar with and adept at using certain key learning actions, the quality of each subsequent performance will improve. Students will be *learning how to learn.*

2. *Certain learning actions, or competences, apply to the teaching/learning environment regardless of the age of the learner or the content being taught.*	The five performance-based learning actions coupled with continuous assessment and evaluation are applicable to all ages and in all content areas. The current level of competence with these learning actions will vary from student to student. There will be a considerable range of competence with these learning actions even within a single classroom or grade level. The focus of improvement is on comparison to a learner's last best effort, not comparison of students to one another and not on the content alone. Performance-based teaching and learning will focus on what students can *do* with what they *know.*

3. *Successful people are able to apply certain key actions to every learning challenge. These actions have similar characteristics regardless of the challenge.*	When students learn, apply, and continuously improve in the learning actions, they are practicing for life after they leave school. Schools must allow students to practice for the challenge, choice, and responsibility for results that they will encounter after "life in school" is over. The more competent students are with a range of these learning actions, the more successful they will be in dealing with the diverse issues, problems, and opportunities that await them.

4. *The problem with the future is that it is not what it used to be.*	Today's informational and technological challenges mean that schools must restructure themselves around a different set of assumptions about what students need to *know* and be able to *do.* Many educators and parents are reaching the conclusion that much of the information we ask students to remember and many of the skills we ask them to practice may no longer be appropriate or useful by the time they leave school. At this point, we ask the question, "If covering content is not enough anymore, what *should* schools be focusing on?" We believe the answer is "The learning actions."

THE PERFORMANCE-BASED LEARNING ACTIONS WHEEL

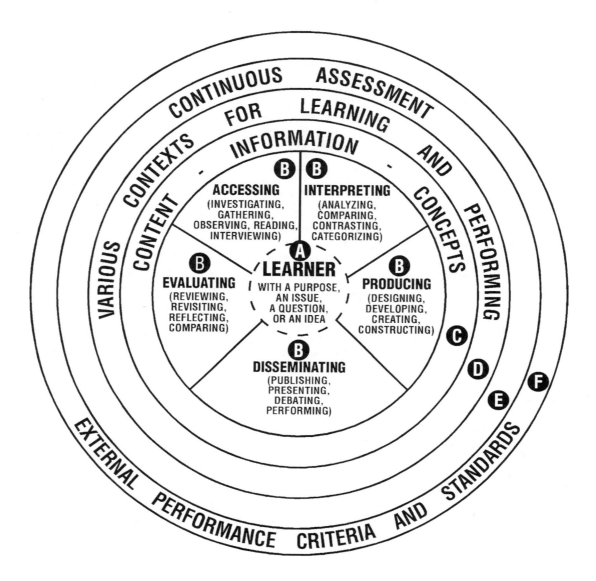

FIGURE 1.1 THE LEARNING ACTIONS WHEEL

Ⓐ The Learner

The learning actions are learner centered and brain based. At the center of the Wheel in Figure 1.1 is the learner with a stimulus for learning. That stimulus may be an issue, idea, or question that may have been suggested to the teacher by the content standards, or it may be something of particular interest to the learner. The learner is in the center because no matter how important we think the content is, it is inert until we add action to it. Everything "revolves" around the developmental levels, the motivation, and the engagement of the learner in the learning actions.

❸ The Five Major Learning Actions of a Performance

The learning actions include five major stages that learners will move through during any performance process. Let's look at the meaning and importance of each.

Accessing

What do I need to know?

How can I find out?

A performance begins with an issue, a problem, or interesting "lead." The learner accesses the information he or she needs to have in order to successfully perform. This information can come from a variety of experiences—but it must come from somewhere. Traditionally, information has come solely from the teacher or the next chapter in a textbook. In today's information-based environment, students must be adept, self-directed learners, determining what is needed and having a wide range of competences for accessing critical information and resources. Learners may investigate, gather, observe, read, and interview, to name a few actions. Whatever actions they engage in to find out what they need to know, *relevant* information must be accessed if the performance is to be as powerful as possible. Accessing is an important first step to a performance and a critical component of success as a learner in any role in or outside school.

Interpreting

What does all of this mean?

So what?

Critical reasoning, problem finding and solving, decision making, and other similar mental processes are what we must do as a part of any important learning that we intend to use in some way. Here, we must make sense of the information we have accessed and decide which information to keep, expand on, or ignore. This component of a performance asks us to analyze, compare, contrast, and categorize—to somehow meaningfully organize the information to represent what we think it all means. This component is critical to a performance process. It clearly determines the level of sophistication and competence with which we can deal with the amount of information constantly vying for our attention and time both in and outside a formal learning situation.

Producing

How can I show what I know?

What impact am I seeking?

Who is my audience?

The producing component of a performance is when we translate what we have learned into a useful representation of our learning. What gets produced represents a learner's competence with design, development, creation, and construction—something tangible that pulls the learning together in some form. This component is the acid test of a learner's competence as a quality producer, a critical role for working and living in the 21st century. In life after school, what we produce usually has a focus, an audience in mind. A powerful performance will always have a clear purpose in mind, a reason for the performance, and an impact that is desired as a result of the performance.

Disseminating

What is the best way to communicate what I have produced?

How can I have an impact on this audience?

How will I know that what I've produced has had an impact?

The fourth learning action of the performance process is disseminating. At this point, we are asking the learners to communicate what they have learned and produced to someone, either directly or indirectly. This is also where the value of an authentic context, someone to be an involved and interested audience, is so apparent. Only in school does there seem to be a lack of attention paid to such a critical motivation for learning and demonstrating. This is truly the point at which learners are dealing with the challenges of a performance setting. Students may publish, present, debate, or perform in a variety of fine and dramatic arts activities, to name a few possibilities. Service learning projects, community performances, and a variety of related school celebrations of learning are all ways for the learning to hold value that may not be inherently present in the simple existence of content standards.

Evaluating

How well did I do?

Where will I focus my plans for improvement?

The evaluation component represents the culmination of one performance and perhaps the launching of another performance cycle. It is the point at which a judgment is made and plans are developed for improvement next time. The quality criteria (in the performance benchmarks) for all the learning actions are the guides for these evaluations. The performance benchmarks in this framework represent the personal evaluation component of ongoing learning and performing on a day-to-day basis, or the self-efficacy of the learner.

ⓒ Content–Information–Concepts

The learning actions are applied to the content–information–concepts identified by the educational system as being essential. Addressing information that is organized around major concepts allows the learner to work with a much broader chunk of information. Thus, the learner is afforded the opportunity for making more connections and linkages and developing greater understanding.

In this text, the selected information has been aligned with the best thinking of current experts representing the National Council for the Social Studies.

ⓓ Various Contexts for Learning and Performing

A context for learning refers to the setting in which the learning occurs, or the audience or recipient of the fruit of the learning or the situation—any of which create a reason, purpose, or focus for the learning.

Traditionally, the context for learning for students has been alone in a chair at a desk in a classroom. However, the context can be a river or stream that runs through the community. Students working in groups with engineers from a local plant can be engaged in collecting specimens and conducting experiments from the water to determine effects of manufacturing on the water's purity, so they can submit a report to the company or the Environmental Protection Agency.

ⓔ Continuous Assessment

The continuous assessment portion of the learning actions wheel represents the continuous improvement process that is imbedded throughout each of the other components. An authentic learning community will engage in a supportive improvement process that is less competitive than it is collaborative and cooperative. To *assess* originally meant to sit beside. During key points in each component of the performance process, students will reflect upon their own work and the work of others. The role of the teacher in this process is to ask questions that guide the student's self-assessment and provide specific feedback to the learner about what is being observed. The conditions we create for this reflective assessment on a daily basis will determine the ultimate success students will have with the performance benchmarks.

ⓕ External Performance Criteria and Standards

The outermost circle represents the system's standards and scoring or grading procedures and patterns.

Remember, there are four critical components of a performance. The learning actions represent an organizing tool for a performance. They describe the components of the performance process. The learning actions also represent quality work according to identified criteria. By themselves, the learning actions are of little use. You have to *know* something to *do* something with it. In *Performance-Based Curriculum for Social Studies*, each performance benchmark combines all four components of a performance:

1) Content–information–concepts
2) Competence: learning actions performed by the learner
3) Contexts that create a reason and a focus for the performance
4) Criteria that define a quality performance

1
CONTENT/CONCEPT STANDARDS FOR SOCIAL STUDIES

A SOCIAL STUDIES PERSPECTIVE

Concern for the common good and citizen participation in public life are essential to the health of our democratic system. Effective social studies programs prepare our students to responsibly address the forces that pull our society apart and hold it together. The social studies curriculum and its aligned practices develop the skills, concepts, and generalizations necessary to understand an increasingly complex, challenging, and diverse global village. Critical thinking and responsible decision making that will guide our students as adults rests on application of rational thinking in a wide variety of social and cultural settings that are authentic and relevant.

As students reflect on their own experience in order to construct social understanding and civic efficacy, they will be developing values and assumptions consistent with democratic procedures. All of the fundamental academic disciplines can be integrated and applied in meaningful ways through the context of the social studies and their related disciplines. When taught well, social studies engages students in confronting ethical and value-based dilemmas and issues and in making personal and civic decisions through a process of careful reasoning and caring consideration.

The inevitability of change is one of the major lessons of history. Today's students face an ever-expanding, ever-changing society and must understand the various influences that affect them individually and within the dynamics of societal groups. Through the study of history, geography, government, civics, economics, sociology, and psychology, students must learn how to facilitate the resolution of conflict and struggle, promote tolerance, support continuity and stability, and promote social growth and improvement. Through active participation and contribution, students will examine the importance of being local, national, and global citizens of the 21st century.

GENERAL SOCIAL STUDIES GOALS

The mission of social studies instruction and its several related disciplines is to "promote civic competence for the primary purpose of helping our young people develop the ability to make informed and reasoned decisions for the public good as citizens of a culturally diverse, democratic society in an interdependent world" (1994, Expectations of Excellence). A comprehensive social studies program should provide every child the opportunity to acquire the knowledge, skills, and the beliefs and values needed for competent participation in social, political, and economic life as well as prepare students for the further study of social studies and its related disciplines. Toward these ends, our goals must be to have students

- Value learning within social studies and across its several related disciplines
- Construct reality from a variety of perspectives relative to the "common good"
- Identify, analyze, and solve problems inherent in a multicultural, pluralistic society
- Communicate as a responsible individual and collaborative member of a democratic society
- Participate fully as a community contributor and global citizen of the 21st century

DEVELOPMENTAL CONSIDERATIONS — ELEMENTARY

The elementary curriculum builds on the important learnings young children acquire during infancy and their early preschool years. By school entry, most children have developed basic time, space, and causal understandings. These understandings connect and orient each child within his or her world.

The home environment and relationships with others play a critical role for the young child. New concepts must always be carefully connected with the child's personal experience and with concepts and understandings already acquired. Early primary education in the social studies, therefore, must always begin with the child's concept of the present and his or her relationship in it. Studies expand outward to develop linkages with the larger geographic and culturally diverse community and the world. Studies of historical issues and peoples must also begin with the personal linkages of a child to his or her family, stories of the past, connections to diverse people and places through concepts of self, and awareness of others in relation to wants and needs in a complex world.

DEVELOPMENTAL CONSIDERATIONS — MIDDLE GRADES

The middle grade child's thinking grows as meanings and connections become increasingly abstract. Knowledge and functional communication and acquisition skills build a complex web of understandings, reasoning abilities, and capacity for comparative analyses. A growing need for concrete ways to "show what they know" and to communicate meaningful learning must be supported and encouraged.

Students throughout the middle grades can study a wide range of concepts relating to human history and social development. They are able to investigate specific people and events that have contributed to the evolution of their own society, its values and assumptions, institutions, forms of governance, security and control, as well as those of other societies. Studies of the past and specific periods of history must be brought to life through learning about the personal lives of people and how events affected them. Students are now able to place themselves within a historical and contemporary context. Learning that results in personal and collaborative reflection and evaluation reaps rich rewards for students in the middle grades.

DEVELOPMENTAL CONSIDERATIONS — SECONDARY

The secondary-level student should be able to grasp complex patterns of relationships between historical events, their multiple antecedents, and their consequences considered over time. The secondary school social studies curriculum must provide learning opportunities that challenge students' growing abstract thinking capabilities and ability to relate to contemporary local, national, and global issues and events. Conflict and "community," the workings of political, economic, and sociological systems, and the personal present and future of the student connect and provide multiple rich contexts for continuing to explore and experience values, assumptions, and beliefs.

Students at the secondary level are able to access information and communicate in authentic ways through community service, political action, and association with special interest groups and organizations. In these ways, the contexts that are now available to students provide life-role opportunities to place social studies into practice. Criteria for quality learning now becomes relative to the impact of the learning on the student and on those with whom he or she collaborates. "Making a difference" becomes the bridge from the content/concepts to actual practice in the community and the world.

CONTENT STRANDS

The various social studies and social studies thinking are an integral part of daily life. The purpose of social studies is to expose all students to all areas of social studies to the greatest degree possible and to sufficiently prepare students for competent participation in social, political, and economic life or for further study in social studies or related disciplines. The National Council for the Social Studies (NCSS) has identified 10 separate but connected and interactive strands in the social studies. The performance benchmarks presented in this text are designed to address each of these strands and their related standards at each of four levels. These 10 strands are

- Culture
- Time, continuity, and change
- People, places, and environments
- Individual development and identity
- Individuals, groups, and institutions
- Power, authority, and governance
- Production, distribution, and consumption
- Science, technology, and society
- Global connections
- Civic ideals and practices

These 10 strands and the standards that accompany them are designed to address the overall curriculum design and comprehensive student performance expectations of a social studies program of excellence. Specific discipline standards in the areas of civics and government, history, economics, geography, and global education can be obtained from their respective professional organizations. These more specific discipline standards provide enhanced content detail for that discipline and support the further development of a quality instructional program.

CONTENT/CONCEPT STANDARDS

The content presented in the performance benchmarks is not intended to be a complete, detailed list of all the information students should know but rather represents essential ideas, concepts, and categories of social studies information and skills. Educators should consider these examples as a guide for their own selection process as they relate these concepts and suggestions to local- and state-identified curricula and expectations relative to contemporary and historical issues and perspectives.

Each of the 10 social studies strands is identified, briefly described, and then presented in terms of what students should be able to know and do by the end of Grades 3, 5, 8, and 12. Each strand will be introduced by a listing of the content/concept standards considered critical to that strand at each of these four grade levels.

PERFORMANCE BENCHMARK FORMAT

The performance benchmarks are sample demonstrations designed with content, competence, context, and criteria that students should accomplish individually and collaboratively by the end of identified grade levels. For each of the 10 strands, there will follow four performance benchmarks. There will be one benchmark for each of the following developmental levels: 3rd, 5th, 8th, and 12th grade. Because these benchmarks represent different developmental levels, they should serve as guides for all teachers from kindergarten through 12th grade. The performance benchmarks are designed to represent a description of what could be expected from a student in a high-quality performance who has a high degree of understanding of the specific content/ concept standard and has consistently experienced the learning actions.

The following template, along with descriptions, is offered as an advance organizer for the performance benchmarks that follow in the next section.

PERFORMANCE BENCHMARK FORMAT

A. SOCIAL STUDIES STRAND AND STANDARD NUMBERS		G. TECHNOLOGY ICON
B. KEY ORGANIZING QUESTION:		
C. KEY COMPETENCES	D. KEY CONCEPTS AND CONTENT	E. PERFORMANCE TASKS
		PERFORMANCE TASK I: PERFORMANCE TASK II:
F. QUALITY CRITERIA: "LOOK FORS"		

A. Social Studies Strand and Standard Numbers

This serves to identify the selected social studies strand and the specific standard numbers chosen from the content/concept standards pages that precede each set of benchmarks.

B. Key Organizing Question

Each performance benchmark addresses specific content information and is organized around a key organizing question. This question serves as a focusing point for the teacher during the performance. The teacher and student can use these questions to focus attention on the key concept/content and competences required in the performance task.

C. Key Competences

The key competences represent the major learning actions of accessing, interpreting, producing, disseminating, and evaluating. These major learning actions are discussed in detail on the preceding pages.

The actions identified are what the student will *do* with the key concepts and content in this benchmark performance. Those do's or learning actions engage students in demonstrations of competence in technical and social processes. Teachers must teach students how to operationalize these learning actions.

D. Key Concepts and Content

The information contained in this section identifies the major concepts that embrace the essential content and knowledge base that was taught and is now addressed in this performance benchmark. These concepts correspond to the standard numbers in Section A above.

E. Performance Tasks

Each performance task requires students to apply the designated content using specific learning actions they have been taught. This is done in a context or situation related to the key question. The performance tasks can be done individually or collaboratively. In either case, it is still the teacher's responsibility to look for the presence or absence of the quality criteria in action.

There are two performance tasks identified on each performance benchmark page to offer teachers a choice or serve as a parallel task for students. Both tasks correspond to the identified quality criteria.

F. Quality Criteria: "Look fors"

The quality criteria represent key actions that students are expected to demonstrate during the performance task. The criteria also guide the teachers and serve as "look fors" during the performance task. In other words, the teacher observes the students for these specific criteria.

These criteria embody the key competences or learning actions that students should have been taught in preparation for this performance task. Students demonstrate the learning actions in connection to the key concepts.

The criteria serve as a process rubric that guides the design of both instruction and assessment. They also serve as a signpost for the learners.

The criteria are identified following a "do + what" formula, which makes it easy to "look for" them.

G. Technology Icon

The presence of a technology icon at the top of a performance benchmark page means there is a corresponding example in the Technology Connections section. These examples indicate how technologies can assist students in carrying out the key competences required in the performance task.

CULTURE

Content/Concept Standards

Students should experience a wide variety of cultures and obtain an understanding of the function of cultural systems and the ways in which cultures exhibit similarities and differences. Exploration and explanation through a wide variety of disciplines (geography, history, anthropology, sociology, psychology, the arts) and themes empower students to develop connections and conceptual understandings regarding the influence of cultures and cultural diversity from a variety of contemporary and historical perspectives.

What students should know how to do by the end of Grade 3

Students observe, listen to, and explore similarities and differences among individuals and groups. They are beginning to develop a range of personal and second-hand experiences from their formal learning relative to cultures and cultural diversity. They are interacting and noticing differences among themselves and want to know more about others. Students should be able to

1. Respond appropriately and retell information acquired through listening, reading, or visual media about differences and similarities among individuals and groups

2. Give examples of how information may be interpreted differently by people with diverse experiences and frames of reference

3. Describe and explain how stories, art, music, and folktales tell about and influence behavior of people from a particular culture

4. Observe and compare how people from different cultures deal with their physical environment and social conditions

5. Give examples of the importance of cultural unity and diversity within and across groups

What students should know how to do by the end of Grade 5

Students actively explore and ask questions about differences among themselves and others relative to the cultural diversity within which they live and attend school. Their experiences prompt questions about the nature of culture and specific aspects such as language and beliefs. Students should be able to

1. Describe and compare similarities and differences among individuals, groups, societies, and cultures and how people of difference cultures respond to needs and concerns

2. Explain how experiences may be interpreted differently by people from diverse cultural perspectives and frames of reference

3. Describe how language, stories, music, and folktales serve as expressions of culture and influence the behavior of people living in a particular culture

4. Compare and contrast ways in which people from different cultures think about and respond to their physical environment and social conditions

5. Give examples and describe the importance of cultural unity and diversity within and across groups

What students should know how to do by the end of Grade 8

Students are formally researching and analyzing a wide range of issues arising from cultural diversity and cultural differences affecting human behavior. Belief systems such as religion and political ideals are explored for clues to influence on other aspects of culture. Students should be able to

1. Compare and explain similarities and differences in the ways groups, societies, and cultures meet human needs and concerns

2. Analyze and explain how information and experiences may be interpreted by people from diverse cultural perspectives and frames of reference

3. Explain and describe how language, literature, the arts, and artifacts demonstrate beliefs and values and contribute to the transmission of culture

4. Analyze and explain how and why individuals and groups respond to their physical and social environments and/or changes to them on the basis of shared assumptions, values, and beliefs

5. Articulate the implications of cultural diversity and cohesion within and across groups

What students should know how to do by the end of Grade 12

Students are understanding and using complex cultural concepts such as adaptation, assimilation, and acculturation drawn from anthropology and sociology to explain how cultural systems function. They are able to collect and analyze data and disseminate information about culture and cultural diversity, conduct reasoned arguments, and reflect on implications and effects of contemporary and historical issues. Students should be able to

1. Analyze and explain how groups, societies, and cultures address human needs and concerns

2. Collect and analyze how data and experiences may be interpreted by people form diverse perspectives and experiences

3. Design products and artifacts that demonstrate understanding of culture as an integrated whole and explain the interactions of language, literature, traditions, beliefs and values, and behavior patterns

4. Compare and analyze patterns for preserving and transmitting culture and for adapting to environmental and social change

5. Describe and interpret values and attitudes that pose obstacles to cross-cultural understanding

6. Construct reasoned analyses about specific cultural responses to persistent human issues

7. Apply ideas and theories drawn from anthropology and sociology relative to persistent issues and social problems

Social Studies:
Grade 3

Performance
Benchmark

CULTURE
CONTENT/CONCEPT STANDARD 4

KEY ORGANIZING QUESTION:

How are individuals and groups alike and different?

KEY COMPETENCES	KEY CONCEPTS AND CONTENT	PERFORMANCE TASKS
Collect Analyze Categorize Create Present Explain	Differences and similarities among individuals and groups. Weather and geography can affect people in a particular geographic region.	**PERFORMANCE TASK I:** Your class will investigate the influences of weather and geography on people in particular regions. You must collect photos, advertisements, and art from a variety of magazines and media that identify different types of dress, homes, work, food, and leisure/sports activities one might find in various regions of the United States. Select three characteristics to show how the people in the pictures are alike and different. Analyze and categorize the unique details of these characteristics. Create a poster to show how the weather and geography in each region might be reasons for these differences. Present and explain your poster and ideas to a group of students in your class.

QUALITY CRITERIA:
"LOOK FORS"

• Identify your task.
• Decide how and where to gather needed information.
• Select most useful information.
• Prioritize the selected information.
• Create a representation of your ideas.
• Plan your presentation.
• Present and explain your findings.

PERFORMANCE TASK II:

As an investigative reporter, develop questions you can use to learn about the cultural heritage or ancestral background of different students in your class. Use your questions to collect information about the origin of the last names of students in your class. In which country did the name originate? What brought these people to the United States? Analyze the collected information by categorizing it. Create a poster to show how one family came to the United States, where they came from, and why they left their country. Present and explain your poster to another team of students in your class.

Social Studies:
Grade 5

Performance
Benchmark

CULTURE
CONTENT/CONCEPT STANDARDS 1, 2

KEY ORGANIZING QUESTION:

How do people interpret their experiences based on their cultural perspectives and frames of reference?

KEY COMPETENCES	KEY CONCEPTS AND CONTENT	PERFORMANCE TASKS
Research Compare Contrast Summarize Conclude Write Present	Experiences are interpreted differently and people respond differently based on the nature and specific aspects of their culture.	**PERFORMANCE TASK I:** You will research information first about the United States and then about a foreign country. Include information related to beliefs, religion, food, homes, government, geography, clothing, and family life of the country you have chosen. Compare and contrast the information with that of the United States. Summarize your information in a written report from the point of view of someone who has recently moved to the United States from the foreign country you researched. Include descriptions of how the person reacts to new experiences in each of the above areas of research, describing how they are interpreted through the cultural background of the person from the foreign country. Summarize your conclusions, and present your report to your parents and then to your classmates.

QUALITY CRITERIA:
"LOOK FORS"

- Identify your purpose clearly.
- Use a variety of resources.
- Identify the main points or categories.
- Select common ideas and ideas that differ.
- Create your major topics and provide necessary details.
- Clearly state your conclusions.
- Organize your ideas in writing.
- Edit for clarity and correctness.
- Present your findings to your audience.

PERFORMANCE TASK II:

As a cultural investigator, research how stories, music, and folktales reach and tell people about the culture of their country. Compare and contrast these types of expression from two different cultures. Summarize your information in a written report. Include examples from each culture, and describe how the stories, music, and folktales differ from each other, including what you think they teach and tell about each culture. Present your summary and conclusions in a report to a group of students in your class or members of a visiting class.

Social Studies:
Grade 8

Performance
Benchmark

CULTURE
CONTENT/CONCEPT STANDARDS 2, 4

KEY ORGANIZING QUESTION:

How do differences within various aspects of culture contribute to conflict across cultures?

KEY COMPETENCES	KEY CONCEPTS AND CONTENT	PERFORMANCE TASKS
Select

Investigate

Analyze

Conclude

Determine

Create

Present | Differences in values and beliefs can explain how conflicts occur among cultures. | **PERFORMANCE TASK I:**
As an investigative reporter, select a current event in which two cultures are in conflict. Investigate the history, initial cause, and development of the event. Analyze the conflict from the two points of view including your conclusions regarding the beliefs and values being expressed from each cultural perspective. Determine how an understanding of the two cultures might help resolve the conflict. Create an enactment of the discussion that might occur between two ambassadors as they use their understanding of each other to work toward reconciliation. Present your enactment to an audience of older students.

PERFORMANCE TASK II:
Within small teams, select an aspect of culture that can be tracked across several cultures: beliefs, values, religion, drama, art, music, dress, and so forth. Investigate the different ways in which cultures demonstrate the aspect your team has selected. Analyze how the differences could create conflict across two or more cultures. Determine why the conflict might occur. Create a depiction of your conclusions, and present your information to another team. |

QUALITY CRITERIA:
"LOOK FORS"

• State your purpose clearly.
• Use a variety of resources.
• Identify the major categories of information.
• Review the ideas from different viewpoints.
• Identify possible conflicts.
• Select possible solutions.
• Develop your enactment or depiction.
• Review for possible additions/deletions.
• Rehearse and share with your audience.

Social Studies:
Grade 12

Performance
Benchmark

CULTURE
CONTENT/CONCEPT STANDARDS 5, 6

KEY ORGANIZING QUESTION:

How does discrimination affect cultural survival, then and now?

KEY COMPETENCES	KEY CONCEPTS AND CONTENT	PERFORMANCE TASKS
Interview Compare Summarize Conclude Depict Discuss	Discrimination and cross-cultural conflict are responses to differences across cultural boundaries. Culture is preserved by maintaining cultural unity, often at the expense of cultural understanding.	**PERFORMANCE TASK I:** Interview people from three different cultures within your community or school. Find out in what ways they may have experienced discrimination, how they felt, how they reacted, and how their culture influences their response to discrimination. Identify and compare the differences across the three cultures. Draw conclusions about how cultures protect themselves from outside discrimination. Summarize your conclusions in an original piece of art. Present and discuss your art and what it means with a small selected audience from the community or a community agency.

QUALITY CRITERIA:
"LOOK FORS"

• Establish clear goals for your project.
• Research various positions on your topic.
• Develop clear, concise questions for your interviews.
• Collate information gathered.
• State your personal conclusions clearly.
• Plan and create your depictions.
• Hold a discussion on your findings.

PERFORMANCE TASK II:
You are a member of an interview team, engaged to find out how you can resolve conflicts at your school that may be caused by cultural differences and cultural identity. Collect suggestions from classmates on what they think could be done to avoid and resolve conflicts across cultures. Compare the responses, and summarize them in a chart or other depiction that clearly shows trends and preferences. Present and discuss your findings and what they mean with a selected group of students from another class.

TIME, CONTINUITY, AND CHANGE

Content/Concept Standards

As students investigate their own historical roots and locate themselves in time, the central focus should be to empower students to reconstruct the past, develop a historical perspective for interpreting the present, and develop an informed perspective on the future. Personal stories and concrete experiences lead to more abstract concepts and deeper understanding of social issues; historical thinking as a set of skills for studying the past; and an understanding of how past, present, and future events are reflected through patterns of change over time.

What students should know how to do by the end of Grade 3

Students at this level are developing their own points of view about events and discovering that interpretations of the same event may vary from person to person. They are developing a concept of time and cause-and-effect as variables in events that directly affect them. Learning is relative to authentic experiences and hands-on application Students should be able to

1. Observe and describe events in a variety of ways
2. Use a wide range of vocabulary to accurately describe time relationships
3. Describe change and how it affects and is affected by people and events
4. Construct simple timelines and depict relationships of people and events across time
5. Investigate and use a variety of sources of information about the past to support a point of view
6. Describe differences in points of view "then and now"

What students should know how to do by the end of Grade 5

Students can reconstruct and represent time and cause-and-effect relationships from second-hand experiences through reading, observing, and listening. Sources can now be identified, located, and researched to gather information about historical events and causal relationships. Students are learning that people from different times and places view the world differently and that change is constant and inevitable. Students should be able to

1. Explain different points of view to describe events in history and support conclusions with evidence
2. Describe and interpret events in relation to time periods and explain cause-and-effect relationships resulting in change
3. Compare and contrast differing accounts of the past and explain how these accounts influence today's understanding and conclusions
4. Use a wide range of resources to reconstruct the past, including interviews, visual depictions, art, music, and folklore
5. Construct representations that demonstrate an understanding of people's differing views of the world over time and in different places
6. Make decisions and evaluate personal actions using elements of historical inquiry

What students should know how to do by the end of Grade 8

At this level students are now able to describe events and points of view across time and to support conclusions and interpretations with reliable sources. Patterns across history are now used to reconstruct the past, understand the attitudes and values that influenced people in different contexts, and predict outcomes of contemporary issues based on those patterns. Students should be able to

1. Investigate and describe theories of history and change and evaluate evidence to support the theories
2. Analyze and explain patterns of history applying concepts such as change, conflict, and causality

3. Describe key historical periods, explain growth and breakdown of cultures and systems, and support conclusions

4. Apply processes for validating sources, investigating causality, and weighing evidence in reconstructing the past

5. Critically analyze attitudes, values, and behaviors of people in different historical contexts

6. Use concepts drawn from history to inform decision making and action on public issues and conflict resolution

What students should know how to do by the end of Grade 12

Students are increasingly critical of the interpretations placed on historical events across time. Complex patterns, connections, and diverse viewpoints can now be systematically interpreted and judged critically. Historical inquiry is used to inform opinions and evaluate contemporary public policy issues. Students should be able to

1. Demonstrate understanding of history as a social construction that influences questions asked and evidence selected to describe events throughout history

2. Explain, analyze, and support conclusions regarding connections and patterns of historical change and continuity

3. Describe and explain significant patterns and periods of change such as cultures and civilizations, and social, political, and economic revolutions

4. Apply processes of critical historical inquiry to reconstruct and reinterpret the past weighing evidence, supporting claims with facts, and validating causality

5. Interpret a variety of historical and contemporary viewpoints related to events and issues, and demonstrate empathy, skepticism, and critical judgment

Social Studies:
Grade 3

Performance
Benchmark

TIME, CONTINUITY, AND CHANGE
CONTENT/CONCEPT STANDARDS 2, 3, 6

KEY ORGANIZING QUESTION:

How can we describe how people are changed by time and events?

KEY COMPETENCES	KEY CONCEPTS AND CONTENT	PERFORMANCE TASKS
Select Determine Construct Describe Explain Display	Interpretations of events vary among individuals and groups. People change over time due to events in their lives.	**PERFORMANCE TASK I:** Select a picture of an adult or senior citizen from a magazine or a newspaper. Determine the approximate age of the person in the picture. Construct a timeline beginning approximately the time you think the person was born. Describe in writing on the timeline several key events in history that might have affected that person as he or she grew and matured. Label the key ideas. Explain how you think key events at the time might have affected that person's development or growth. Display your timeline and story.

QUALITY CRITERIA:
"LOOK FORS"

• Clearly state the purpose of your investigation.
• Identify key factors.
• Review possible plans for your creation.
• Provide clear details and important information.
• Organize your ideas.
• Present information and supporting visual.

PERFORMANCE TASK II:
As a historical investigator, select an event in history that affected large numbers of people. Determine how the event might have affected people present at the event. Construct a visual description of someone's experience as that person might have experienced the event. Share your visual with a classmate, and explain how the person learned from the event, how they felt about it, and how their lives changed. Display your visual depiction for others to view.

**Social Studies:
Grade 5**

**Performance
Benchmark**

TIME, CONTINUITY, AND CHANGE
CONTENT/CONCEPT STANDARDS 1, 2, 5

KEY ORGANIZING QUESTION:

How do people interpret the same events differently?

KEY COMPETENCES	KEY CONCEPTS AND CONTENT	PERFORMANCE TASKS
Choose Research Compare Contrast Write Illustrate Report	Change is constant and inevitable; history is a series of cause-and-effect relationships; history is interpreted in many different ways.	**PERFORMANCE TASK I:** As a team of newswriters, choose a current event and research the facts and accounts of the event from a variety of sources. Compare and contrast the various accounts. Write your own account of the event, focusing on the information that is consistent across your sources. Include illustrations that show what happened in your account of the event. Report about your event to another team. **PERFORMANCE TASK II:** You are to choose a current event and research the facts and accounts of the event from a variety of sources. Compare and contrast accounts of the event from a range of sources, including newspapers, magazines, television, and other media. You are to write an account of the event as though it happened one 100 years ago. Include illustrations of the event. Report to history students how the event could be misinterpreted based on the passage of time and changing opinions.

QUALITY CRITERIA:
"LOOK FORS"

- Clearly state your selected event.
- Gather information on the event from a variety of valid resources.
- Select key ideas.
- Analyze the accounts for likenesses and differences.
- Explain your understanding in writing.
- Create an illustration to support ideas.
- Organize ideas and report to others.

Social Studies:
Grade 8

Performance
Benchmark

TIME, CONTINUITY, AND CHANGE
CONTENT/CONCEPT STANDARDS 1, 2, 3, 4

KEY ORGANIZING QUESTION:

How is history both documented and "altered" based on a combination of fact, opinion, bias, and point of view?

KEY COMPETENCES	KEY CONCEPTS AND CONTENT	PERFORMANCE TASKS
Collect Categorize Label Create Teach	Historical accounts are determined and influenced by bias and point of view. Reliability of sources varies and evidence must be weighed carefully in reconstruction of the past.	**PERFORMANCE TASK I:** Collect information about a current event in the news. Include as many sources and differing points of view as you can find. Categorize and then label the different points of view. Do some types of media have a particular slant or point of view? Create a chart that depicts the variety of positions according to bias or point of view. Include quotes, news articles, pictures, and other sources of support on your chart by category. Teach the concepts of bias and point of view to another class.

QUALITY CRITERIA:
"LOOK FORS"

- Clearly state your purpose.
- Decide how and where to gather information.
- Include information from a variety of contributors.
- Separate and label according to points of view.
- Select a direction or plan.
- Develop a chart.
- Teach understanding to others in an organized manner.

PERFORMANCE TASK II:

As a team of historical investigators, you will collect examples of current and historical political cartoons. Categorize and then label the symbols and images the cartoonist uses to influence the point of view and opinions of the observer. For example, animals such as skunks to depict crooked politicians, and so forth. Create a chart that depicts cartoons over time according to the symbols and use your chart as a visual to teach what you have learned to students in another class.

Social Studies:
Grade 12

Performance
Benchmark

TIME, CONTINUITY, AND CHANGE
CONTENT/CONCEPT STANDARDS 1, 2, 3

KEY ORGANIZING QUESTION:

What are examples of patterns in history, and why are they repeated over time?

KEY COMPETENCES	KEY CONCEPTS AND CONTENT	PERFORMANCE TASKS
Research Analyze Compare Summarize Write Present	History is a social construction that influences questions asked and evidence selected to describe events. History displays significant patterns and periods of change over time.	**PERFORMANCE TASK I:** In small teams, research examples and definitions of the concept *revolution*. Analyze and compare the episodes, events, and key issues that lead to revolution. Individually summarize your conclusions about the pattern of events that lead to revolution, and write a report. Compare your results with results of your teammates. Organize and support your ideas; then summarize and present the ideas of your team to another team.

QUALITY CRITERIA:
"LOOK FORS"

- Clearly define your task.
- Use a variety of reliable resources.
- Identify the key ideas.
- Compare and contrast the various components.
- Prioritize selected information and details.
- Organize information in writing and tie conclusions to original task.
- Evaluate audience response and adjust accordingly.

PERFORMANCE TASK II:
You are to research two countries in which there has been a history of rapid political change. Analyze and then compare these two countries for similar events, issues, leadership, governance, or cultural background that influenced these rapid changes. Summarize the key findings; then write a report using these patterns to look at the United States. What similarities do you see? Does the United States have the potential for rapid change in a similar way to the countries analyzed? Support your response with documented evidence. Present your information to a group in your class.

PEOPLE, PLACES, AND ENVIRONMENTS

Content/Concept Standards

The study of people, places, and human-environment interactions leads students to an understanding of geographic forms and how these forms have affected people in the past as well as in the present. The relationship of environmental contexts to public policy and issues of domestic and international significance are explored through contemporary and historical issues.

What students should know how to do by the end of Grade 3

Personal experience forms the basis for early exploration of geographic concepts and skills. Curiosity about unknown and distant people and places creates a rich context for connecting students' understanding of themselves and their local geography with unfamiliar people and places. Students should be able to

1. Access and describe the earth and its landforms using globes, pictures, and maps

2. Construct a variety of artifacts that demonstrate relative location, direction, size, and shape

3. Use data sources and comparative information to interpret geographic forms and relationships

4. Distinguish and describe geographic features, and weather, climate, and the water cycle

5. Describe the interrelationships of people, the places in which they live, their impact on the environment, and the effects of catastrophic phenomena

What students should know how to do by the end of Grade 5

Increasing knowledge and analytical competence leads students at this level to concrete expression of concern for their local and regional environment. The relationship between human beings and their environment establishes the theme of responsibility for results. Students should be able to

1. Interpret and explain geographic relationships and the development of landforms using globes, pictures, and maps

2. Construct representations of locales, regions, and the world that demonstrate understanding of relative location, direction, size, and shape

3. Use a variety of data sources such as grids, topographic maps, and graphs to describe, interpret, estimate, and calculate relationships and to communicate about geography

4. Describe and speculate about the relationships of weather, climate, and the water cycle

5. Research and describe relationships between culture, ideas, design of living spaces, and geographic location

6. Investigate and analyze social and economic effects of environmental changes and crises, and evaluate and propose alternative uses of resources and land in the community and beyond

What students should know how to do by the end of Grade 8

Students at this level are able to use abstract data and analysis of information to learn and communicate about the physical and cultural environment. Studies at this level evaluate the conflict and collaboration that characterize contemporary issues and expand beyond local experience to diverse cultures. Students should be able to

1. Create complex representations of landforms that demonstrate understanding of relative size, distance, location, and their relationships

2. Use a wide range of data sources and geographic tools to generate, manipulate, and interpret relationships of geography and its inhabitants including density and spatial distribution

3. Explain complex relationships between landforms and their relationships within the ecosystem

4. Analyze physical system changes and geographic patterns associated with weather, climate, and the water cycle

5. Describe relationships between cultural values, beliefs, and ideals and describe the evolution of constructed living spaces, neighborhoods, and community gathering places

6. Interpret and explain how historical events are related to geographic phenomena, describe the effects on social and economic issues, and propose and support alternative possibilities for local, regional, national, and global resources

What students should know how to do by the end of Grade 12

Students in high school are able to apply geographic understanding across a broad range of fields, including the fine arts, science, and humanities. Studies address patterns from the past to the present and the future, and public policy is explored relative to domestic and international issues. Students should be able to

1. Design and construct original representations that communicate complex understanding of geographic relationships and related systems such as weather, climate, the water cycle, and geographic phenomena

2. Describe and differentiate various regional and global patterns including relationships of population density and location

3. Interpret and explain how culture, human needs, government policy, and values and ideals are reflected in the design of constructed living spaces, neighborhoods, and community gathering places

4. Interpret, explain, and evaluate the interaction of people and their environment historically and relative to contemporary issues, including impact of environmental changes and crises

5. Evaluate past and current policies for utilization of resources, and propose alternative policies at the local, regional, national, and global levels

Social Studies:
Grade 3

PEOPLE, PLACES, AND ENVIRONMENTS
CONTENT/CONCEPT STANDARD 2

KEY ORGANIZING QUESTION:

How do people determine and explain their surroundings and locations?

KEY COMPETENCES	KEY CONCEPTS AND CONTENT	PERFORMANCE TASKS
Observe Describe List Design Share Display	Geographic location, direction, size, and shape can be described through mental maps and physical representations.	**PERFORMANCE TASK I:** You are a cartographer who will observe and describe how maps were developed a long time ago. How were places and physical objects shown on these maps? Observe your classroom or school, and list what you see that might be on a map. Design an "old" map that shows key objects including relative size and location. Share your map with others, and display it in your classroom. **PERFORMANCE TASK II:** How would you assist someone to get to your house from your school? On your way to school, observe and list all the places along the way that have been constructed; include stores, shopping centers, fields, houses, and so on. Describe the locations of these manufactured objects on a grid map that shows the relative locations of these constructions. Share your grid map with others, then arrange to display it in one of the locations you depicted on your grid map.

QUALITY CRITERIA:
"LOOK FORS"

- Identify your task and purpose.
- Note the various details.
- Record the needed information.
- Include relevant details.
- Select appropriate information.
- Arrange in a visual representation.
- Edit for needed adjustments.
- Present and explain to another.
- Display appropriately for others to view.

Social Studies: **Performance**
Grade 5   **Benchmark**

PEOPLE, PLACES, AND ENVIRONMENTS
CONTENT/CONCEPT STANDARD 5

KEY ORGANIZING QUESTION:

How do landforms, weather, and geographic features affect where people live
and work?

KEY COMPETENCES	KEY CONCEPTS AND CONTENT	PERFORMANCE TASKS
Investigate Determine Compare/Contrast Summarize Illustrate Teach	Environment and weather systems affect where people live, what they do, and how they construct their homes and work environments.	**PERFORMANCE TASK I:** As a member of an environmental investigation team, you will study a large land mass and determine how the landforms affected irrigation patterns and movement of people to certain areas. Compare and contrast your results with what another team found out about a different land mass. Together you are to summarize the information in an illustration. Then, teach what you have learned to a student from another fifth-grade class.

QUALITY CRITERIA:
"LOOK FORS"

• Identify your purpose.
• Gather information from a variety of resources.
• Organize the essential information.
• Seek similarities and differences with gathered data from
  another student or team.
• Draw conclusions based on your combined data.
• Depict conclusions in a visual representation.
• Teach others what you have discovered.

PERFORMANCE TASK II:
You are to investigate a state and determine the desirable resources, physical attractions, and weather conditions that would encourage people and "investors" to locate in that state. Compare and contrast the state you are studying with a state another student is studying. Summarize your state's advantages in an illustration that you can use to teach another fifth-grade student all you learned about your state.

Social Studies:
Grade 8

PEOPLE, PLACES, AND ENVIRONMENTS
CONTENT/CONCEPT STANDARDS 4, 6

KEY ORGANIZING QUESTION:

How do natural disasters influence the lives of people who experience them?

KEY COMPETENCES	KEY CONCEPTS AND CONTENT	PERFORMANCE TASKS
Research Determine Write Publish	Complex relationships exist between natural phenomena and the people who experience them.	**PERFORMANCE TASK I:** You are an investigative reporter researching the impact of natural disasters on the people who experience them. Using a variety of data sources such as databases, graphs, and media accounts, determine the social and economic effects on a population that has experienced a natural disaster. Write an investigative report, and publish your information for another class or a local reporter. **PERFORMANCE TASK II:** Research a well-known natural disaster such as the Johnstown Flood, the 1906 San Francisco Earthquake, Hurricane Hugo, or another catastrophic environmental event. Using news reports, personal accounts, and depictions of the disaster, determine what the effects were on those who experienced it, and write a first-person account that you can publish for others to read.

QUALITY CRITERIA:
"LOOK FORS"

- Establish purpose and task.
- Gather information from a variety of references and resources.
- Organize and document your information.
- Identify the effects on those involved.
- Record your ideas in a written piece.
- Edit and rewrite for clarity and purpose.
- Organize layout and publish.

Social Studies:
Grade 12

Performance
Benchmark

PEOPLE, PLACES, AND ENVIRONMENTS
CONTENT/CONCEPT STANDARD 4

KEY ORGANIZING QUESTION:

What are the relationships between people and their environments and the effects on culture, dress, food, customs, and values?

KEY COMPETENCES	KEY CONCEPTS AND CONTENT	PERFORMANCE TASKS
Explore Analyze Conclude Explain Speak	The landforms and physical conditions where people live influence their culture, human needs, and values and ideals.	**PERFORMANCE TASK I:** It has been said that "to know a people you must know about their country, natural resources, and landforms." Select a foreign country, and explore this statement in relation to that country. Analyze multiple aspects such as the culture, history, dress, food, and customs. Draw conclusions about the relationships between the various aspects, and explain them in a speech for a 10th-grade social studies class.

QUALITY CRITERIA:
"LOOK FORS"

- Clearly state your goal and purpose.
- Gather necessary information reflecting a variety of viewpoints and resources.
- Compare and contrast the various positions or aspects.
- Draw conclusions based on your gathered data.
- Organize ideas according to purpose.
- Include relevant information and details.
- Use standard conventions for speaking to your identified audience.

PERFORMANCE TASK II:
As a community contributor, select a local issue related to the use of land or resources or the use of tax base to improve, change, or protect an area of land in your community. Explore the points of view expressed through a variety of media. Analyze the information and draw conclusions about the interests, values, and beliefs expressed about the issue. Explain your conclusions in a speech to a local agency or community group that is involved in the issue.

INDIVIDUAL DEVELOPMENT AND IDENTITY

Content/Concept Standards

Students need to be aware of individual development, learning, and growth, and how these are influenced by experience, culture, and society. Personal identity and ethical principles underlying individual action are explored at every level within the contexts of families, peers, schools, and communities. Patterns of human behavior and ethics are investigated through core concepts drawn from psychology, social psychology, sociology, and anthropology.

What students should know how to do by the end of Grade 3

The primary-level student learns about personal wants, and behaviors based on observation and experience. Studies are related to interests; reflections on learning and growth over time; and observation of family members and community members. Students should be able to

1.   Reflect upon and report personal growth and learning over time
2.   Relate self to surroundings
3.   Describe characteristics of nuclear and extended families
4.   Describe how family, groups, and community affect one's daily life
5.   Identify interests, capabilities, and personal needs
6.   Describe responses to events in one's life
7.   Work independently and cooperatively to accomplish goals

What students should know how to do by the end of Grade 5

Students are actively exploring their personal identities within a variety of contexts and situations. At this level students are projecting themselves into the future and can actively set, achieve, and reflect on results and goals. Observational skills related to patterns and differences across age groups increase. Students should be able to

1.   Assess personal learning and growth patterns over time
2.   Distinguish and compare unique characteristics of nuclear and extended family members
3.   Explain how learning and growth affect personal behavior
4.   Describe how family, groups, and community affect personal choices and responsibilities
5.   Interpret and evaluate factors that contribute to one's personal identity and perceptions
6.   Analyze events and identify reasons for various responses among different individuals
7.   Individually and collaboratively choose, plan, implement, and evaluate short-term projects and goals

What students should know how to do by the end of Grade 8

The middle-level student can focus on social and cultural influences on personal behavior. Students are confronting many issues of choice, responsibility, and consequences of group association. Intense focus on personal wants and needs and awareness of group differences provides rich opportunities for authentic learning contexts. Students should be able to

1.   Evaluate and relate one's characteristics, perceptions, personality, and learning patterns to selection and achievement of personal goals
2.   Compare and contrast family, gender, ethnicity, nationality, and institutional affiliations to personal identity and influence on one's daily life
3.   Describe and relate personal changes and beliefs to social, cultural, and historical contexts and events

4. Identify and interpret examples of stereotyping, conformity, and diversity issues

5. Individually and collaboratively develop, structure, implement, and evaluate short- and long-term projects and goals

What students should know how to do by the end of Grade 12

Methods and strategies from studies of psychology and sociology and theoretical constructs for individual development and identity are applied to past, present, and predicted future situations. The high school student is able to determine and examine personal goals for the future and develop complex plans for achievement of those goals. Study focuses on contemporary society, its systems, and its impact on individuals and groups. Students should be able to

1. Use knowledge of one's characteristics, perceptions, personality, and learning patterns to determine and describe goals relative to life role and career aspirations

2. Explain and represent personal connections to historical and contemporary contexts and systems including how family, ethnicity, gender, and other group and cultural influences contribute to a sense of self

3. Interpret the impact of ethnic, national, and cultural influences on specific situations and events

4. Design, structure, implement, and evaluate short-and long-term projects individually and within groups and institutions

5. Investigate and interpret factors that affect mental health and behavioral disorders in contemporary society

Social Studies:
Grade 3

INDIVIDUAL DEVELOPMENT AND IDENTITY
CONTENT/CONCEPT STANDARDS 1, 3, 5

KEY ORGANIZING QUESTION:

What are the characteristics that can describe one's family history and its effects on life today?

KEY COMPETENCES	KEY CONCEPTS AND CONTENT	PERFORMANCE TASKS
Interview Summarize Describe Write Publish Share	One's family has unique characteristics that can be described and that explain certain traits and tendencies.	**PERFORMANCE TASK I:** You are a family health investigator who will interview members of your family about their health histories, beginning with yourself. Summarize your findings, and describe how your future health history might be affected. Publish your findings and predictions in a "Family Health Newsletter" that you can share with your family.

PERFORMANCE TASK II:

Interview two members of your family to find out what they think you share with them in behaviors, traits, and physical characteristics. Summarize the information from each interview. Describe the differences and similarities of the information in a "How My Family Sees Me" brochure. Publish and share the brochure with your family.

QUALITY CRITERIA:
"LOOK FORS"

- Identify clear goals.
- Prepare clear, concise questions for your interview.
- Select the main topics.
- Identify the supporting details.
- Describe in detail your findings and thoughts.
- Organize your information in writing.
- Publish in a newsletter or brochure.
- Present and explain to your family.

Social Studies:
Grade 5

Performance
Benchmark

INDIVIDUAL DEVELOPMENT AND IDENTITY
CONTENT/CONCEPT STANDARDS 1, 3

KEY ORGANIZING QUESTION:

How has my learning and experience over time affected my personal identity?

KEY COMPETENCES	KEY CONCEPTS AND CONTENT	PERFORMANCE TASKS
Identify Analyze Create Discuss	Interests, capabilities, and perceptions are affected by experience, learning, and growth over time.	**PERFORMANCE TASK I:** As a personal historian, Identify two or three key events in your life. Analyze your reaction to the events and how they continue to affect your thinking and behavior today. Create a timeline of the events. Discuss your timeline and your analysis with another member of your class.

QUALITY CRITERIA:
"LOOK FORS"

• Establish your purpose and goal.
• Select two or three personal events.
• Review them for patterns.
• Connect the patterns in your personal behaviors/actions.
• Develop a plan for your process/product.
• Review and adjust as needed.
• Share in detail with a small group.

PERFORMANCE TASK II:

Think about important decisions and changes you have made in your life. Identify a few of those decisions and choices, and analyze them for how you made those decisions. Can you see a pattern? Create a "decision-making process" that describes the steps you take when you make a decision, and discuss your process in a group.

Social Studies:
Grade 8

Performance
Benchmark

INDIVIDUAL DEVELOPMENT AND IDENTITY
CONTENT/CONCEPT STANDARDS 3, 5

KEY ORGANIZING QUESTION:

How do individuals cope with conflicts between their value systems and conditions created by environmental influences and situations created by others?

KEY COMPETENCES	KEY CONCEPTS AND CONTENT	PERFORMANCE TASKS
Investigate Analyze Develop Propose Plan Present	Mental problems as well as positive coping mechanisms are the result of learning to cope with internal conflicts between values and external influences and conditions.	**PERFORMANCE TASK I:** Many mental health and emotional problems are due to conflicts between social influences and one's personal value system. Investigate a type of mental illness such as depression, schizophrenia, or psychotic behavior, and analyze the environmental issues that might influence the development of this mental health problem. Develop and propose a plan for how the community could prevent the development of these influences. What support systems might be helpful? Present your plan to a representative from a local health agency, a mental health professional, or a social worker.

PERFORMANCE TASK II:

As a member of a team, investigate information from local health and social service agencies about self-help groups, crisis help lines, and other support systems available in your local community. Analyze the collected information, and develop a proposal for students your age to easily access these services if they are needed. Present your plan to the school nurse or a visiting social service professional.

QUALITY CRITERIA:
"LOOK FORS"

- Clearly state your purpose.
- Gather pertinent information from a variety of valid resources.
- Organize the gathered information according to your purpose.
- Include essential details.
- Identify a meaningful sequence.
- Expand your key ideas.
- Extend to the fullest possibility.
- Select appropriate method of communicating with your audience.
- Use standard conventions of public speaking.

Social Studies:
Grade 12

Performance
Benchmark

INDIVIDUAL DEVELOPMENT AND IDENTITY
CONTENT/CONCEPT STANDARDS 2, 3, 5

KEY ORGANIZING QUESTION:

How does stereotyping influence relationships among individuals and across groups?

KEY COMPETENCES	KEY CONCEPTS AND CONTENT	PERFORMANCE TASKS
Interview Determine Summarize Chart Depict Compare Conclude Write	Differences in culture, values, and diversity issues can lead to conflict among individuals and across groups.	**PERFORMANCE TASK I:** You are to interview several students in your class, school, or community representing a variety of ethnic, cultural, and racial backgrounds. Determine how they experience you and other groups in different ways, stereotypes they have of other groups, and how they believe conflicts among different groups arise. Summarize the results of your interviews in a chart or other data depiction, and compare your results with the results reached by a classmate. Draw a personal conclusion, and write an editorial for the local paper on this issue.

QUALITY CRITERIA:
"LOOK FORS"

- Establish clear goals.
- Prepare focused, concise, and thoughtful questions.
- Record and organize your gathered information.
- Identify the key ideas.
- Select important supporting details.
- Arrange and lay out the essential information.
- Share and exchange ideas with a classmate.
- Review your initial and final personal position.
- Present your ideas in written form.

PERFORMANCE TASK II:
You are a social scientist who will interview a number of people representing differing cultural backgrounds and ethnically diverse groups about a current local or national issue that is in debate in the media. Determine how opinions and attitudes differ among individuals. Summarize your information and conclusions in a chart or other depiction, and compare your results with a fellow classmate's results. Discuss your findings, and then draw a personal conclusion. Write an article reflecting your opinion for a school or class paper.

INDIVIDUALS, GROUPS, AND INSTITUTIONS

Content/Concept Standards

Students need to understand how institutions and organizations influence our lives and reflect the core social values of those who comprise them. Examination of the role of the individual in creating, maintaining, and changing institutions contributes to identification and understanding of institutional change for the common good. How people organize themselves around common needs, beliefs, and interests is approached through the behavioral sciences and social theory and leads to the study of how tensions develop when goals, values, and principles conflict among social and political institutions.

What students should know how to do by the end of Grade 3

The primary-level student needs to identify and examine institutions that directly affect his or her life. How schools, clubs, and other groups influence them and how they in turn influence formal and informal groups are the authentic contexts for students at this level. Students should be able to

1. Identify roles in group situations
2. Give examples of groups and institutions and their purposes
3. Cite experiences of conflict between a group/institution and personal or group beliefs and values
4. Describe how groups and institutions further continuity and change

What students should know how to do by the end of Grade 5

Students need to explore how institutions form and maintain themselves in response to beliefs, wants, and needs within society. At this level students need to understand that institutions are formed and controlled by individuals based on core values and that institutions cooperate and conflict with one another. Students should be able to

1. Explain concepts of role within group situations
2. Describe how behavior patterns are learned through group membership and modeling
3. Explain how individual beliefs and belonging to more than one group can cause personal conflict
4. Identify and describe examples of how groups and institutions can both promote and prevent furthering the common good

What students should know how to do by the end of Grade 8

At the middle level, students explore how institutions change over time, promote social conformity, and respond to individual and group needs. This is a time to pursue institutional membership for promotion of the common good. Students should be able to

1. Use concepts of role, status, and social class to describe institutional and group affiliations
2. Explain how groups and institutions influence people, events, and culture
3. Identify and analyze examples of conflict between individual beliefs and institutional efforts to promote social conformity through laws and governmental policies
4. Participate in group and institutional membership and articulate reasoned choices

What students should know how to do by the end of Grade 12

High school students are actively involved in institutional life and pursuing understandings of historical and contemporary issues around the paradigms and traditions that support both stability and change through institutions and groups. Social theory and behavioral sciences are applied to authentic situations. Students should be able to

1. Apply concepts of role, status, and social class in describing the interactions and connections between individuals and groups/institutions in historical and contemporary settings

2. Explain historical and contemporary relationships between people, events, and cultures and connections to group/institutional changes over time and in relation to concepts of the common good

3. Analyze examples of conflict between individual beliefs and efforts to promote social conformity by groups and institutions

4. Apply theories and inquiry processes from behavioral sciences and social psychology to the interpretation and representation of current issues and social problems

Social Studies: **Performance**
Grade 3   **Benchmark**

INDIVIDUALS, GROUPS, AND INSTITUTIONS
CONTENT/CONCEPT STANDARDS 1, 2

KEY ORGANIZING QUESTION:

What does the term "community contributor" mean?

KEY COMPETENCES	KEY CONCEPTS AND CONTENT	PERFORMANCE TASKS
Gather Define Develop Describe Share	Individuals influence groups and institutions by their behavior and the roles they play.	**PERFORMANCE TASK I:** Identify a person in your school community who helps the school function better. Gather information about this community contributor, and define the meaning of these two words. Then, develop a description and a criteria for a community contributor. Use the criteria to describe yourself as a contributor in your school community, and share your results with a partner. Do you fit the criteria? What would you have to do to fit the criteria?

QUALITY CRITERIA:
"LOOK FORS"

- Identify your purpose.
- Decide where and how to collect information.
- Use several resources for information.
- Identify your main ideas.
- Develop a clear description.
- Share your information with your partner.

PERFORMANCE TASK II:
Gather examples you find in newspapers and magazines about people you believe are community contributors. Define the term, and develop a description of a community contributor. Select a person you know, and share with the class what you think this individual does that makes him or her a community contributor.

Social Studies:
Grade 5

INDIVIDUALS, GROUPS, AND INSTITUTIONS
CONTENT/CONCEPT STANDARDS 1, 2

KEY ORGANIZING QUESTION:

How do groups and institutions affect the behavior of individuals?

KEY COMPETENCES	KEY CONCEPTS AND CONTENT	PERFORMANCE TASKS
List Catagorize Develop Chart Recommend Justify	Groups and institutions can both promote and prevent furthering the common good through its rules and roles.	**PERFORMANCE TASK I:** List all the rules and required behaviors in your school. Categorize them according to rules you think are good and rules you think are unnecessary or not in the best interests of your classmates and the school. Develop a chart that shows what you think and your recommendations. Justify changes as you present to another group in your classroom. **PERFORMANCE TASK II:** As a team of community designers, your group will list rules and roles that a perfectly operating community would have. Categorize your information according to major aspects of your community. Develop a chart that shows your information. Then make recommendations and justify them to another group of "designers."

QUALITY CRITERIA:
"LOOK FORS"

• Clearly state your purpose.
• Brainstorm your lists.
• Organize the lists into categories.
• Arrange your information on a chart.
• Extend the information and recommendations.
• Support your recommendations with examples.

INDIVIDUALS, GROUPS, AND INSTITUTIONS
CONTENT/CONCEPT STANDARDS 2, 3

KEY ORGANIZING QUESTION:

How do organizations form, and how do they influence society?

KEY COMPETENCES	KEY CONCEPTS AND CONTENT	PERFORMANCE TASKS
Select Collect Analyze Design Write Present	Individuals, groups, and institutions change society through membership and influence. Organizations form based on events and perceived needs among groups in society.	**PERFORMANCE TASK I:** Select an event in history that resulted in the formation of an organization that changed the course of an event or influenced society. Collect information about the history and development of the organization, and analyze how and why the organization was formed. Design a visual and written description of the event. Organize and present your results to a government class or to a local chapter of this organization.

PERFORMANCE TASK II:
Select a local community organization, and collect information about the organization from brochures, articles, and reports about its purpose and work. Analyze the key aspects of this organization, and then, using it as a model, design a community organization, create its brochure, and write an article that describes an effect your "organization" can have on the community. Then, present your materials to a group of students from another class.

QUALITY CRITERIA:
"LOOK FORS"

- Identify your task and purpose.
- Identify possibilities for your focus.
- Identify your target.
- Generate materials from a variety of sources.
- Use a variety of strategies to compare and contrast.
- Select appropriate information for your purpose.
- Create a representation with necessary details.
- Organize thoughts in writing.
- Present materials and ideas to targeted group.

Social Studies:
Grade 12

Performance
Benchmark

INDIVIDUALS, GROUPS, AND INSTITUTIONS
CONTENT/CONCEPT STANDARDS 2, 3

KEY ORGANIZING QUESTION:

How does persuasion through the media influence individual, group, and institutional behavior?

KEY COMPETENCES	KEY CONCEPTS AND CONTENT	PERFORMANCE TASKS
Select Analyze Design Persuade Present	Contemporary and historic issues can be examined using behavioral science and social psychology.	**PERFORMANCE TASK I:** Political cartoons influence opinions about institutions and events. Select a variety of historic and contemporary political cartoons. Analyze how the cartoonist influences opinion and how images and strategies are used. Design a political cartoon that uses similar images and strategies to persuade a viewer to adopt the opinion illustrated in your cartoon. Present your cartoon to an artist, a cartoonist, or a group of students.

QUALITY CRITERIA:
"LOOK FORS"

- Clearly establish your purpose.
- Gather necessary resources.
- Analyze and organize the information according to strategies and influence.
- Select appropriate information/ideas.
- Create a representation.
- Poll the viewpoints represented in your audience.
- Convince them of your opinion.
- Check for shifts in opinion.

PERFORMANCE TASK II:

As a political "spin doctor," you will select a current hot topic. Analyze the issues, and design a persuasive speech that includes a variety of strategies intended to persuade. Present your speech to a key group, and persuade them to shift their opinion toward your point of view.

POWER, AUTHORITY, AND GOVERNANCE

Content/Concept Standards

Students explore their natural and developing sense of fairness and order as they experience relationships with others. These early understandings lead to deeper learnings about the structures of power, authority, and governance through contemporary and historical issues within the United States and throughout the world. Through political science and law, students learn about concepts of security and order and explore the complex concepts of rights and responsibilities in a just society.

What students should know how to do by the end of Grade 3

Themes of fairness, rights, and responsibilities emerge as students examine their own experiences at home and at school. Exploration and examples of these basic concepts extend to a range of familiar contexts and themes. Students should be able to

1. Discuss and describe personal rights and responsibilities as a member of a family, peer group, and school class

2. Explain the purpose of government and create depictions of relationships between government agencies

3. Give examples of how organizations promote unity and diversity in order to maintain order and security

4. Describe how differing needs and wants lead to disputes and create need for order and security

What students should know how to do by the end of Grade 5

Examples of early meaningful concepts expand to include government and its authority as well as illuminations of these concepts through historical and contemporary stories. Students are now learning about the influence of key historical and contemporary leaders and organizations. Students should be able to

1. Describe how government provides for security and maintains order

2. Develop representations that describe the relationships among local, state, and national government and the roles of leaders in these agencies

3. Use examples to explain how cooperation and conflict arise and are addressed by government

4. Explore the role and impact of technological advances in a variety of examples of power, authority, and governance

5. Interpret and evaluate how the wants and needs of the individual and groups relate to concepts of fairness, equity, and justice

What students should know how to do by the end of Grade 8

Increasingly abstract information and applications lead to analysis of the role and features of government and how order and security are established and maintained in the United States and throughout the world. Motivations, conditions, and actions that address the themes of power, authority, security, and control are examined in relation to individual and group rights and responsibilities. Students should be able to

1. Examine issues related to the individual and the common good

2. Analyze how governmental powers are used and abused historically and in contemporary times

3. Explain how balance is achieved through governmental systems

4. Describe how governments respond to conflicting needs and wants around the forces of unity and diversity

5. Design and explain basic features and concepts of the political system in the United States

6. Explain how technology has influenced, contributed to, and resolved conflict within and among nations

7. Describe how governments apply basic concepts of power, authority, and governance to contemporary issues and problems

What students should know how to do by the end of Grade 12

Students use abstract principles to study the various systems that have developed in the context of power, authority, and governance. Historical and contemporary issues are examined, and active participation in local and national discussion and debate begins in earnest. Students should be able to

1. Analyze and evaluate issues and examples of use and abuse of personal rights and responsibilities

2. Explain how government acquires, uses, and justifies its powers

3   Examine and contrast how nations and organizations have dealt with internal and international issues of conflict and collaboration

4. Compare a variety of political systems and ideologies to the United States and analyze and evaluate applications of these political systems

5. Apply ideas and theories from political science to the examination of historical and contemporary issues and problems

6. Propose, prepare, present, and defend an analysis of public policy before a juried panel

Social Studies: **Performance**
Grade 3   **Benchmark**

POWER, AUTHORITY, AND GOVERNANCE
CONTENT/CONCEPT STANDARDS 1, 3

KEY ORGANIZING QUESTION:

How do organizations develop unity and "commitment" among their members?

KEY COMPETENCES	KEY CONCEPTS AND CONTENT	PERFORMANCE TASKS
Collect Clarify Design Develop Display Explain	Organizations promote unity and diversity to maintain order and security. Symbolic organizational strategies create "a sense of belonging and order" to members of organizations and to the outside world.	**PERFORMANCE TASK I:** Organizations and communities use logos and easy-to-remember statements to bring unity and "commitment" to the people who belong to them. Collect a variety of sample logos and mission statements. Then, in small teams, clarify how you would bring your team together with a unified message and logo. Involving everyone in the process, design a logo and develop a mission statement that your team can remember. Display your logos and mission statements for the entire class, and explain your thinking to a group of classmates.

QUALITY CRITERIA:
"LOOK FORS"

• Identify your purpose.
• Plan your actions to involve others.
• Clearly identify the steps.
• Review all possibilities.
• Create a representation.
• Supply necessary details of language.
• Assemble your materials for believing.
• Present your information to your audience.

PERFORMANCE TASK II:
You are community organizers of an imaginary new community called "Diverseville." Your new community has a variety of members with different wants and needs and backgrounds. How will you bring your community together? Collect ideas from all the students in the class. Clarify how you will motivate everyone to be an active member of Diverseville. Design and develop a community "unity" plan that includes everyone's ideas and suggestions. Display the Diverseville Organizational Plan on the walls of your classroom, and explain how you came up with your plan to another class.

Social Studies:
Grade 5

POWER, AUTHORITY, AND GOVERNANCE
CONTENT/CONCEPT STANDARD 2

KEY ORGANIZING QUESTION:

What are the relationships between local, state, and national government?

KEY COMPETENCES	KEY CONCEPTS AND CONTENT	PERFORMANCE TASKS
Research Read Interview Analyze Illustrate Depict Describe	The relationships between levels and types of government agencies affect the power and authority of those agencies. Understanding these relationships is critical to citizenship and community participation.	**PERFORMANCE TASK I:** Research and read information about a local, a state, and a national government agency, identifying what they do. Interview someone from one of these agencies who can help you analyze how these agencies relate to one another. Illustrate the types of work and decisions made by each agency. Depict all the connections using an organizational design strategy. Describe your representation to a government teacher or someone who works in one of these agencies. **PERFORMANCE TASK II:** As an investigative journalist, you are to research and read information about a government agency in your community. Interview someone from that agency, and acquire details about what the agency does, the names of its key departments and what they do, and why this agency is important to the people and community. Analyze your findings, and decide how you would improve the work and organization of the agency. Illustrate and depict a representation of your improvements, including how the organization operates now and how it would be different. (Use different colors, symbols, etc. to show the two representations.) Describe your representations and improvements to another class or government employee.

QUALITY CRITERIA:
"LOOK FORS"

• Clearly state your purpose.
• Develop essential questions you will address.
• Gather necessary information from a variety of resources including key people.
• Organize your information.
• Compare and contrast what you discovered with other possibilities or ways of functioning.
• Create a visual representation.
• Explain your ideas to your identified audience.

Social Studies:
Grade 8

Performance
Benchmark

POWER, AUTHORITY, AND GOVERNANCE
CONTENT/CONCEPT STANDARDS 2, 4

KEY ORGANIZING QUESTION:

How do we use formal debate and argument to resolve issues of differences of opinion in a democratic form of government?

KEY COMPETENCES	KEY CONCEPTS AND CONTENT	PERFORMANCE TASKS
Investigate Clarify Prepare Debate Evaluate	Debate and deliberation inform opinion and form political influence in the United States.	**PERFORMANCE TASK I:** Debate is a time-honored form of communication used to influence public opinion in the United States. An effective debater will prepare not only for his position but will have considered what the other side's arguments will be. You are to choose one side of the intense debate about more versus less government intervention in local issues. Investigate the rules and standards for a debate. Clarify and state the different viewpoints. Prepare your side of the debate according to the standards. Include supportive facts for your opinions and conclusions. Hold your debate for an audience that will assess your performance. Then repeat your debate and reverse sides. Argue for the other side of the issues. Evaluate the effect and the usefulness of this strategy. **PERFORMANCE TASK II:** Talk shows are a popular venue for debate. As political talk show guests, your team is going to choose a current issue being debated in the media. Investigate how talk shows are formatted and what makes them interesting to listeners and observers. Investigate information on the points of view being expressed on your topic in the media. Clarify and state the different viewpoints. Prepare an overview of the debate and an introduction for the talk show. Your team will then present an active and engaging debate, covering all sides of the issue and including convincing support for each point of view. You may wish to have "call-in" questions to add more authenticity to your presentation. Evaluate the interest level of your debate as compared to the talk shows you investigated.

QUALITY CRITERIA:
"LOOK FORS"

- Clearly identify your focus and purpose.
- Gather the necessary information from a variety of reliable resources.
- Select important topics.
- Derive interpretations and connections on the topics.
- Develop a clear representation of ideas.
- Present positions clearly with supporting details.
- Review procedure and ideas.
- State a summarizing opinion.

Social Studies:
Grade 12

Performance
Benchmark

POWER, AUTHORITY, AND GOVERNANCE
CONTENT/CONCEPT STANDARDS 1, 2

KEY ORGANIZING QUESTION:

How can we make informed decisions and influence the decisions our government makes that affect our ability to meet our individual needs and wants?

KEY COMPETENCES	KEY CONCEPTS AND CONTENT	PERFORMANCE TASKS
Select Collect Analyze Develop Recommend Write Persuade	Individuals influence decisions made by government. Government makes choices that influence our ability to meet our needs and wants.	**PERFORMANCE TASK I:** Government makes choices, sometimes unpopular choices, about the use of resources such as tax money, environmental issues, priorities for land use, and so forth. As a responsible citizen, how can you ensure that you are informing yourself about the decisions your government is making? Select a popular local or national issue in which there is much disagreement about what the government should do. Determine how you can collect and select information that is as unbiased as possible and how you can then express your opinion to those who will be making a decision. Develop a recommendation, and write a persuasive letter to encourage those decision makers to consider your point of view. Deliver your letter.

QUALITY CRITERIA:
"LOOK FORS"

- Clearly identify an issue.
- State your purpose.
- Decide how and where to gather information.
- Choose appropriate materials.
- Prioritize the main ideas.
- State major points clearly.
- Include necessary details.
- Derive a personal opinion.
- State an alternative possibility.
- Convey ideas in writing.
- Engage emotion to convince others.

PERFORMANCE TASK II:

Select a prominent recent issue that has been argued in the courts and that was decided by citing one of the constitutional amendments. Collect and select information on the amendment being addressed, and write an analysis that demonstrates your understanding of the critical issues cited in the court's decision as well as the influence of the amendment on that decision. If you were to recommend an additional amendment, what would it be? Develop a recommendation for an amendment, and write a persuasive letter to the Supreme Court. Include your reasons for the amendment, and explain how it would improve the justice system in the United States.

PRODUCTION, DISTRIBUTION, AND CONSUMPTION

Content/Concept Standards

Students investigate their own experiences relative to personal wants and needs and how the consequences of their decisions affect themselves, other groups, and the communities in which they live. These initial concepts develop a strong base for eventual study of the allocation and distribution of land, labor, capital, and management from complex local, state, national, and global perspectives. Core principles that influence decisions about what to produce, organization for production, distribution, and allocation of the factors of production become a recurring theme as students expand their knowledge of economics and sociopolitical systems.

What students should know how to do by the end of Grade 3

Initial concepts develop from understandings of wants and needs and how conflict can arise from personal differences. As students explore these concepts, they can extend their experiences to groups, communities, the nation, and beyond. Students should be able to

1. Identify and make choices from among available options with an understanding of abundance and scarcity
2. Define and distinguish between needs and wants
3. Explain and demonstrate concepts of mine, yours, ours, theirs, and so forth
4. Identify producers and consumers at the school, family, and community levels
5. Describe interrelationships of workers, specialization, and how goods and services are exchanged
6. Demonstrate relative costs and concepts of price to supply and demand through charts, graphs, and displays

What students should know how to do by the end of Grade 5

Basic economic principles develop at this level. Students can examine and evaluate priority uses of limited resources, estimating needs and production requirements for classroom projects and programs. The basics of supply, demand, distribution, and consumption are explored in authentic ways through the economics of the classroom and the community. Students should be able to

1. Explain how our economic decisions are affected by abundance and scarcity including how price is affected by supply and demand
2. Describe and show examples of private and public goods and services
3. Depict the interrelationships among a variety of examples of institutions that make up our economic systems
4. Analyze the role of money in our lives
5. Explain local and national events using economic concepts
6. Select an issue and apply economic concepts to suggestions for solutions

What students should know how to do by the end of Grade 8

Middle-level students expand their application of economic principles to reasoned processes around fundamental questions of production and allocation of resources. Themes and investigations support the development of an economic perspective to personal and collective issues. Students should be able to

1. Depict how abundance and scarcity are influenced by economic systems
2. Explain how supply, demand, price, incentive, and profit are related to each other, how they affect what is produced, and how distribution occurs in a competitive market system

3. Interpret and explain how personal and collective values and beliefs influence economic decision patterns using authentic examples and stories

4. Compare basic economic systems and show how decisions differ as to what is produced, to whom it is distributed, and how it is consumed

5. Select a contemporary issue and compare a variety of solutions using economic principles

What students should know how to do by the end of Grade 12

At this level students study economic and sociopolitical systems and examine historical and contemporary issues of policy and practice. Applications and role performances range from classroom and school-based investigations to sophisticated examination of international production and control of resources through the Internet and other information-accessing tools. Students should be able to

1. Investigate and explain how abundance and scarcity of goods and services require economic system intervention

2. Analyze costs and benefits to society of private versus public allocation of goods and services

3. Analyze and evaluate the roles and relationships of economic systems and predict future issues and changes in selected systems

4. Compare economic systems across various societies and contrast them to one another addressing values, beliefs, and cultural factors that affect them

5. Interpret and explain the relationship between domestic and global economic systems

6. Evaluate historic and contemporary issues through application of core economic principles

Social Studies:
Grade 3

Performance
Benchmark

PRODUCTION, DISTRIBUTION, AND CONSUMPTION
CONTENT/CONCEPT STANDARDS 2, 4

KEY ORGANIZING QUESTION:

How can we distinguish between needs and wants when we make choices for consumption?

KEY COMPETENCES	KEY CONCEPTS AND CONTENT	PERFORMANCE TASKS
Select Investigate Collect Interview Analyze Determine Chart Explain Share	Individual choices are driven by needs and wants. Marketing influences our choices for consumption of goods and services.	**PERFORMANCE TASK I:** Candy, cookies, and sugar-rich foods have been declared an unhealthy and unnecessary addition to our diets. And yet, more money is being spent on these "fad-fat" foods than on many healthier foods combined. You are to select and investigate one of these unhealthy foods, analyze your findings, and determine why it sells so well. Collect advertising, costs, and display information, and interview experts including consumers and market managers. Chart the factors that influence buying habits. Explain the results of your findings. Share your information with a group of student consumers.

QUALITY CRITERIA:
"LOOK FORS"

- Identify your purpose.
- Collect a variety of data related to your purpose.
- Include information from interviews.
- State your conclusions clearly.
- Create a quality chart that distinguishes differences and includes accurate, detailed information.
- Present your findings using concise language.

PERFORMANCE TASK II:

You are going to be a "clever consumer." You are to select several types of well-known products that are commonly advertised in newspapers and magazines. Collect advertising "deals" such as coupons, price comparisons, and sales information. Interview clever consumers like your parents, relatives, and other shoppers. Analyze your findings, and determine where the best values can be obtained and which are within reasonable distance. Explain what you have learned about being a clever consumer. Chart the aspects you used to determine best values. Share your information with your parents and other students.

Social Studies:
Grade 5

Performance
Benchmark

PRODUCTION, DISTRIBUTION, AND CONSUMPTION
CONTENT/CONCEPT STANDARDS 1, 3

KEY ORGANIZING QUESTION:

What are the relationships among the factors of abundance and scarcity of goods and services, supply and demand, and decisions to produce and distribute?

KEY COMPETENCES	KEY CONCEPTS AND CONTENT	PERFORMANCE TASKS
Choose Compare Depict Write Explain Recommend Share	Economic system structures play a large part in determining what is produced and distributed in a competitive market system.	**PERFORMANCE TASK I:** Products go through multiple hands before they arrive in a store to be purchased by customers. You are to choose an example of a product such as a car, an electric tool, a home appliance, and so on. Choose a product that goes through several stages in its production. Describe the components of production with an illustration, a chart, a timeline, or another visual depiction. Include a written explanation of each stage of production. What might be reasons for this production process instead of another possibility? Develop a second visual that shows how you would improve the process of production, thereby reducing production time and cost. Compare the differences between the two, and write a description of the comparison and your recommendations. Share your results with another class. **PERFORMANCE TASK II:** You are a member of a community planning committee making decisions about limited land availability. You have a proposal by local citizens to develop a playground and park. They have delivered thousands of signatures in support of the land use. Now, a national manufacturing firm has just announced that it is bringing 2,000 low to middle income jobs into the community due to expansion of its production facilities just outside town. You are faced with a choice of building an apartment complex to house new employees or moving ahead with the original proposal. How will you make the decision? What information do you need to collect? Describe how supply and demand, prices, incentives, and profits play a part in the final decision. Using charts, graphs, and other comparative information, develop a written decision. Explain and share your decision and recommendations for resolution of conflicts of wants and needs to a "citizens' committee" of students in your classroom.

QUALITY CRITERIA:
"LOOK FORS"

• Select and identify essential information for your task.
• Identify and examine the main topics or components.
• Represent your ideas using appropriate materials.
• Organize your ideas in writing with clearly stated details.
• Explain your conclusions.

Social Studies:
Grade 8

Performance
Benchmark

PRODUCTION, DISTRIBUTION, AND CONSUMPTION
CONTENT/CONCEPT STANDARDS 2, 3, 4

KEY ORGANIZING QUESTION:

How are decisions made about the impact on the United States of increasing relationships with foreign countries?

KEY COMPETENCES	KEY CONCEPTS AND CONTENT	PERFORMANCE TASKS
Research Analyze Conclude Justify Present	Decisions to engage in coproduction and trade with other countries are influenced by different and sometimes conflicting beliefs and values.	**PERFORMANCE TASK I:** Research the history of trade and developing relationships with one of the United States' foreign manufacturing or trading partners (China, Mexico, Japan). How did the relationship develop? What are the costs/benefits of the relationship for the United States? Analyze the various points of view in relationship to becoming dependent on another country for meeting needs and wants of the United States. Draw conclusions about what you have learned, and prepare a speech that you will present to a panel of history/government students urging either a continued or a changed relationship. Include your reasoned and justified opinion in your presentation.

QUALITY CRITERIA:
"LOOK FORS"

- Identify a clear purpose.
- Use a variety of resources.
- Select the most appropriate information for the purpose.
- Analyze the information by comparing and contrasting the main ideas.
- Support conclusions with evidence.
- Present and explain your position.

PERFORMANCE TASK II:
Production and distribution of consumer goods has often been a source of conflict within and among countries of the world (favored-nation status for China, Japanese trade restrictions, etc.). As a team, research an example in which resources and the desire for those resources have resulted in armed conflict. Using a timeline and "causality webbing" to analyze the development of the conflict, trace the issues and event leading to armed conflict. Draw conclusions about points at which the conflict could have been avoided, and include justification for your conclusions. Prepare a speech to present to another team using your visual information.

Social Studies:
Grade 12

Performance
Benchmark

PRODUCTION, DISTRIBUTION, AND CONSUMPTION
CONTENT/CONCEPT STANDARDS 3, 4, 6

KEY ORGANIZING QUESTION:

What are the major concepts across time that we can use to compare and analyze current issues and decisions in production, distribution, and consumption?

KEY COMPETENCES	KEY CONCEPTS AND CONTENT	PERFORMANCE TASKS
Interview Research Analyze Contrast Write Discuss	Economic concepts and patterns repeat themselves throughout history and across contemporary national and international issues. These concepts can be used to predict and explain many problems that arise in relationships within and across countries of the world.	**PERFORMANCE TASK I:** The United States has had extensive experience with the causes and effects of a crisis of supply and demand over the past 200 years. In the role of an investigative journalist, you are to interview someone who experienced one of these crises — WWII, the energy crisis of 1973, oil embargoes during the war with Iraq, and so forth. Research the issues and opinions that were expressed about the causes, effects, and solutions to the crisis at the time. What were the personal conflicts and concerns that arose from the curtailment of resources according to the person you interviewed? Write a journal article to be included in a class journal of the various examples of these crises of supply and demand. Compare and contrast the similarities and differences among the examples, and discuss the patterns and concepts shared by these crises in a discussion with the class.

QUALITY CRITERIA:
"LOOK FORS"

- State your problem clearly.
- Design questions for gathering information.
- Study a variety of reliable resources on your topic/problem.
- Use a variety of strategies to compare and contrast the gathered information.
- Select the most appropriate information for your purpose.
- Organize information logically and clearly in writing.
- Present your findings and review ideas with others.

PERFORMANCE TASK II:

Select two countries from each of two major continents that have had a history of trade relations with each other over a period of time. In small teams, research the development of the relationship between the two countries. You will then be interviewed and in turn interview two other "expert teams." Determine which major economic concepts and system patterns are illustrated by the development of the relationships and shared by two pairs of countries you learned about. Compare and contrast the information you received from the two experts, and write an analysis of your conclusions. Discuss your results with another team.

SCIENCE, TECHNOLOGY, AND SOCIETY

Content/Concept Standards

Many of our most difficult social choices are related to technology. Students learn how technologies have involved and altered the course of history. Critical questions of control versus humans' quest for knowledge and the implications of these decisions and who should make them are explored through natural and physical sciences, social sciences, and the humanities. Questions about who should benefit from technology and about the preservation of our fundamental values and beliefs in an interdependent world are drawn from a wide variety of issues and fields of study.

What students should know how to do by the end of Grade 3

Students explore how technologies influence their lives. They trace technology through time and identify evolutionary and revolutionary examples. The experiences of students bridge to how others are affected and will be affected in the future by technology. Students should be able to

1.   Identify examples of technology in their lives

2.   Investigate how technology has changed over time and how it has affected the lives of people and communities

3.   Describe choices resulting from scientific and technological advances and identify values and beliefs these choices represent

4.   Identify laws and policies that affect the use and abuse of technology

What students should know how to do by the end of Grade 5

Explorations begin to connect to issues of values, beliefs, and how choices and priorities are made around technological advances. Examples are used to analyze from a variety of perspectives. Students should be able to

1.   Describe technological advances and how they have affected people's lives in a variety of contexts

2.   Explore and depict how physical environments have been changed by technological advances

3.   Explain how technology has affected our values, beliefs, and attitudes about our world and our lives

4.   Propose solutions to issues of monitoring of technological uses and abuses

What students should know how to do by the end of Grade 8

Middle-level students are expanding their concepts to what is possible in the future and how technology has changed and will shake our beliefs about what is possible. Students are investigating potential and opening fields of study using technological advances. Students should be able to

1.   Analyze and explain how people's lives and perceptions have changed in relation to technological advances

2.   Describe how regulation might be imposed and justify a reasoned argument identifying guiding values, beliefs, and attitudes upheld in the argument

3.   Propose ethical solutions to the dissonance between scientific advances and social norms and values

What students should know how to do by the end of Grade 12

At the high school level, students are connecting their career explorations and choices to needs for competence with technology. They are investigating and confronting contemporary issues around the ethics of such technological breakthroughs as life extension, personal privacy, and genetic engineering, and the role of the individual, institutions, and governmental controls in these breakthroughs. Students should be able to

1. Describe and depict the interdependence of science, technology, and cultural factors using examples from historical and contemporary societies

2. Evaluate a variety of positions and policies around the use and abuse of scientific advances and technology

3. Develop strategies and design approaches for influencing public opinion associated with technology and ethical choices

Social Studies:
Grade 3

Performance
Benchmark

SCIENCE, TECHNOLOGY, AND SOCIETY
CONTENT/CONCEPT STANDARD 2

KEY ORGANIZING QUESTION:

What is technology, and how does it affect you?

KEY COMPETENCES	KEY CONCEPTS AND CONTENT	PERFORMANCE TASKS
Observe Develop Categorize Select Write Summarize	Technology affects all of us and has done so throughout recorded history.	**PERFORMANCE TASK I:** Observe examples of technology around your home and your school. Develop a list of all the technology you use on a daily basis. Categorize the various uses of technology (transportation, communications, etc.), and sort your list into those categories. Select one list of items, and decide not to use any items on that list for one day. After your experiment, write about your experience. What was impossible to avoid (the school bus or electricity, etc.)? Decide how you depend on that particular technology. Summarize your conclusions in a "letter to a friend." **PERFORMANCE TASK II:** As a technology investigator, you are to look for examples of how technology is used. Develop a list of all the technology examples you observe in one day. Select one category represented on your list and develop the history of it. Create a timeline representing the key ideas. Tell why this technology is important today. Share your ideas with another class and tell about the timeline.

QUALITY CRITERIA:
"LOOK FORS"
- Clearly state your purpose.
- Collect a variety of samples.
- Categorize the collected examples.
- Identify your personal focus.
- Select the main points about your selection.
- Identify important details about each point.
- Condense the information into a letter/report
- Tell an audience about your experience and information.

Social Studies:
Grade 5

Performance
Benchmark

SCIENCE, TECHNOLOGY, AND SOCIETY
CONTENT/CONCEPT STANDARDS 1, 2

KEY ORGANIZING QUESTION:

How does supply and demand influence the development of technological advances?

KEY COMPETENCES	KEY CONCEPTS AND CONTENT	PERFORMANCE TASKS
Observe Collect Analyze Decide Summarize Conclude Present	Wants and needs affect the development of technological experimentation and advances.	**PERFORMANCE TASK I:** As a technology investigator, you are to observe and collect information from the media about advances in health care and cures. After 2 weeks, you are to analyze your information for the advances that are making the most news. Decide which individuals and groups will benefit most from the advances. Draw conclusions and summarize them in a report that includes specific information that supports your opinions. Present your conclusions to another science class or to a local expert in health such as the school nurse.

QUALITY CRITERIA:
"LOOK FORS"

- Identify and clearly state your purpose.
- Select where and how you will observe and what information you will obtain.
- Identify the various aspects of your obtained information.
- Select the most appropriate ideas for your purpose and prioritize them.
- Identify the audience that will benefit from your findings.
- Summarize your information.
- Clearly state your conclusions.
- Provide supporting evidence.
- Use standard convenience of public speaking when you present to your selected audience.

PERFORMANCE TASK II:

Schools have many of the same environmental problems as any large place where groups work and live together. One of the most common choices to be made is about the use of biodegradable versus cost-effective disposable products. As an investigative reporter, observe and collect information about how this choice is made at your school. Analyze the information and decide what factors have been considered in the choices that have been made. Summarize your conclusions in a report, and present your conclusions to another class.

Social Studies: **Performance**
Grade 8   **Benchmark**

SCIENCE, TECHNOLOGY, AND SOCIETY
CONTENT/CONCEPT STANDARDS 2, 3

KEY ORGANIZING QUESTION:

How can decisions be made about control of the development and use of scientific advancements?

KEY COMPETENCES	KEY CONCEPTS AND CONTENT	PERFORMANCE TASKS
Research Summarize Predict Design Teach	Scientific advances may conflict with societal norms and values.	**PERFORMANCE TASK I:** Many advances in technology are highly controversial. They can often be put to either positive or negative use. Governmental agencies, scientists, and social scientists are concerned about the conflict inherent in many recent advances. Research the development of one such positive/negative technological advancement and trace the development of the scientific and media discussion regarding control for protection of society from potential misuse. Summarize your findings and predictions regarding the eventual applications of the particular advancement in technology. Design a depiction of your conclusions, and teach a lesson on your findings to a class of younger students. **PERFORMANCE TASK II:** DNA testing is becoming an increasingly common approach to determining the facts related to cases involving parentage, rape, crime, and other critical issues of guilt or innocence. And yet many states do not allow DNA evidence to be submitted as evidence in court trials. Research the validity and reliability of DNA testing and the interpretation of results. Compare and contrast the potential for influencing the results of legal cases. Summarize your conclusion, and predict the future of DNA testing in your state. Design a depiction to convey your conclusions. Teach about the information you have collected to a government class.

QUALITY CRITERIA:
"LOOK FORS"

- Identify your topic and focus.
- Gather information from a variety of resources.
- Organize your collected information.
- Provide documentation on your sources.
- Summarize the information according to categories.
- Predict various possible outcomes.
- Design and create a depiction showing your conclusions.
- Teach a lesson based on your findings to an appropriate audience.

Social Studies:
Grade 12

Performance
Benchmark

SCIENCE, TECHNOLOGY, AND SOCIETY
CONTENT/CONCEPT STANDARDS 1, 2, 3

KEY ORGANIZING QUESTIONS:

What is the role and influence of ethics in development and application of technology?
How are policies developed in relation to technology, and who develops these policies?

KEY COMPETENCES	KEY CONCEPTS AND CONTENT	PERFORMANCE TASKS
Identify Determine Justify Conclude Write Present	Public opinion varies widely around issues of technology and ethics. Politics and the media influence decisions about the use and abuse of technology.	**PERFORMANCE TASK I:** Recent widely publicized national court cases have raised the question of the media's role in either limiting or bombarding the public with information that may jeopardize the Bill of Rights' guarantees to a fair and speedy trial. How can a trial be fair if a jury cannot be found that is uninformed about the evidence to be presented? Using a famous case as an example, you are to identify the points of view with regard to policies and practices related to advances in communication technology and its influence on the ethics of "unalienable rights." Determine and write what would be an appropriate policy to protect the rights of individuals in such situations. Justify the limitations that might be placed on the media. Write a position paper reflecting your findings and conclusions. Present your paper to a local expert on policy development or to a representative group from the media.

QUALITY CRITERIA:
"LOOK FORS"

- Clearly state your purpose and focus.
- Identify the various issues or points of view related to your topic.
- Gather needed information of the topic from a variety of sources.
- Draw a conclusion and justify it with supporting evidence.
- Draft, edit, and write a paper on your position.

PERFORMANCE TASK II:
As a career investigator, you are to identify a potential career that involves the use of technology. Determine what issues of ethics would be involved in the possible career. Write a letter to a college where you might receive the necessary training, and obtain information about how the college addresses the issues of ethics. Justify your selection of that college or another based on its treatment of the ethics issues in a written "acceptance" or "refusal" to proceed into the program in question. Present your conclusions to a team of peers, or share with a representative from the registrar's office from a local college.

GLOBAL CONNECTIONS

Content/Concept Standards

Students of today are exposed to firsthand experiences on a global scale through various media and other events. Students need to possess the competence to analyze tensions between national interests and global priorities. Deep understanding of the realities of global interdependence requires the ability to think systematically about personal, national, and global decision making and to initiate responsive action plans. If students are to contribute to the development of possible solutions to our many persistent and emerging issues, they will need to have wide exposure to critical issues such as peace, human rights, trade, and global ecology.

What students should know how to do by the end of Grade 3

Even very young students are exposed to the expanse of differences and conflict across cultures of the world every day through the media. At this level, developing a language for describing differences and similarities and for acknowledging different points of view is paramount. The students should be able to

1. Identify differences between people, cultures, belief systems, and physical environments

2. Investigate and describe causes and consequences of pollution, endangered species, and examples of conflict, cooperation, and interdependence

3. Depict relationships between global concerns and popular solutions

What students should know how to do by the end of Grade 5

Upper primary students are differentiating, defining themselves, and comparing their known contexts in relation to global events and issues. At this level students are identifying basic issues and concerns, and initiating action plans. Students should be able to

1. Describe how art, music, and communication reflect differences across people, cultures, and physical environments and explain how these differences can cause conflict as well as understanding

2. Explain how contemporary issues can be addressed through cooperation and collaboration

3. Analyze and describe how conflict is a function of differences in wants and needs, and a disparity between values, beliefs, and cultural factors

4. Explore examples and proposed solutions to contemporary issues of human rights

What students should know how to do by the end of Grade 8

The middle-level student is analyzing national responses to international and global issues and events. Investigations involve accessing information from a variety of often disparate sources and developing complex solutions to multifaceted problems. Background developed for understanding the differences and interdependencies of a global community is used to balance ethnocentric tendencies. Students should be able to

1. Describe and analyze the effects of changing technologies on people and cultures of the world

2. Explore causes and consequences and describe solutions proposed for emerging issues and global concerns such as health, security, resources, and environmental quality

3. Depict and justify a variety of solutions to bring together disparate global interests

4. Describe the roles of international and emerging multinational organizations

What students should know how to do by the end of Grade 12

At this level students are investigating systemic theories and applications to state, national, and global decisions. Critical issues and ethical dilemmas are investigated and proposals are developed during complex role performances and projects. Students should be able to

1. Use a range of disciplines to explain and pose solutions to current and emerging global tensions and conflicting wants and needs

2. Formulate reasoned and justified policies to address current concerns and issues related to human rights, environmental quality, and territorial disputes

3. Design presentations that illustrate how individual behaviors and decisions connect and conflict with global systems

Social Studies:
Grade 3

GLOBAL CONNECTIONS
CONTENT/CONCEPT STANDARD 1

KEY ORGANIZING QUESTIONS:

How can we find out about other countries and the people who live there?
What questions would we want to ask?

KEY COMPETENCES	KEY CONCEPTS AND CONTENT	PERFORMANCE TASKS
Investigate Identify Compare Contrast Write Describe	Understanding differences between countries, cultures, and physical environments leads to understanding of differing points of view among countries of the world.	**PERFORMANCE TASK I:** You have been asked to be an ambassador to another country during your summer vacation. You need to find out all that you can about the country before you go. Investigate and list all the important information you will need. Identify the customs, history, culture, language, monetary systems, and other important influences, and compare and contrast the country you will visit with the United States. Write a letter to the embassy of the country telling the ambassador why you are looking forward to your visit to the country. Describe specific facts about the country in your letter. Send your letter to the embassy. **PERFORMANCE TASK II:** As a historical investigator, you are to investigate an event in which a foreign country and the United States were in conflict. Identify and list the points of view expressed by each country in relation to the conflict. Compare and contrast the points of view. Include information about the culture, language, geographic location, and other facts about each country that may have contributed to the conflict. Present your position in a letter to your teacher. Describe specific ideas or facts.

QUALITY CRITERIA:
"LOOK FORS"

- Identify your purpose.
- Decide how and where to gather information.
- Collect necessary information.
- Identify key ideas.
- Find the differences.
- Create a letter stating your ideas.
- Include necessary details to support your ideas.
- Send or present your letter.

Social Studies:
Grade 5

Performance
Benchmark

GLOBAL CONNECTIONS
CONTENT/CONCEPT STANDARD 4

KEY ORGANIZING QUESTION:

What are human rights, and what should the United States do about abuses of these rights in other countries?

KEY COMPETENCES	KEY CONCEPTS AND CONTENT	PERFORMANCE TASKS
Select Research Analyze Describe Draft Write Present	Human rights issues exist in many countries, including the United States. There are many differing points of view about involvement and interference by other countries in resolving these issues.	**PERFORMANCE TASK I:** Human rights is considered by many to be an issue affecting people in this country and throughout the world. Our concern for the rights and dignities of others is much of what makes us human. Research examples of human rights. Select a country that has a history of reported human rights abuses. Research the issues addressed, and analyze and describe which human rights are being abused. Draft and write a position paper in which you describe what you think the United States should or should not have done about the abuses. Present your report to another team or class. **PERFORMANCE TASK II:** The United States has a long history of internal conflicts among its citizens. Many of these conflicts have sprung from or resulted from human rights abuses. Research an example in which there have been accusations of human rights abuse within the United States. Select which rights were/are abused and analyze for the differences in culture, customs, and history that may have contributed to the abuse. Draft and write a position paper in which you describe the abuses. Present your paper to a panel of students from another class.

QUALITY CRITERIA:
"LOOK FORS"

- Establish clearly stated purpose.
- Use a variety of resources for information.
- Organize the gathered data.
- Compare and contrast major ideas.
- Include necessary supporting ideas.
- Create a draft of your ideas.
- Develop a written document.
- Share your position paper with an appropriate audience.

Social Studies:
Grade 8

Performance
Benchmark

GLOBAL CONNECTIONS
CONTENT/CONCEPT STANDARD 1

KEY ORGANIZING QUESTION:
How can human rights, environmental protection, and interdependence among communities of the world be addressed during times of rapid global economic development?

KEY COMPETENCES	KEY CONCEPTS AND CONTENT	PERFORMANCE TASKS
Research Determine Design Analyze Conclude Present Justify	Individual and human rights often are in conflict with global and multinational economic development.	**PERFORMANCE TASK I:** The United States has often been accused of exploiting the workers of underdeveloped countries. Designer clothes, toys, fine linens, and many luxury items are made by children and impoverished populations in foreign countries far removed from the targeted customers. You are to research this issue and determine how prevalent the situation is and in which countries this is occurring. Design a data chart showing comparisons of the wages for the workers and profit for the manufacturers/importers of the resulting products. Analyze your data, and present your results and conclusions to another investigative team of students. Justify your conclusion with specific examples of evidence.

QUALITY CRITERIA:
"LOOK FORS"
- Identify the purpose and goal.
- Clearly state investigative questions.
- Identify potential resources.
- Select most useful resources.
- Identify various positions.
- Compare and contrast the approaches.
- Summarize the data.
- Create a detailed visual representation.
- State your position.
- Support with documented evidence.
- Present using standards for your audience.

PERFORMANCE TASK II:
As a policy designer, you are to research an issue currently being addressed by the World Trade Organization. Include data about the positions being taken by various countries in regard to the issue. Determine what the point of view might be for several countries, and then design a data chart showing comparisons of the different points of view. Analyze your collected data, and present your findings and your conclusion to another investigative team of students. Justify your conclusion with specific evidence or examples.

**Social Studies:
Grade 12**

**Performance
Benchmark**

GLOBAL CONNECTIONS
CONTENT/CONCEPT STANDARDS 1, 2, 3

KEY ORGANIZING QUESTION:

How and why do global connections affect us?

KEY COMPETENCES	KEY CONCEPTS AND CONTENT	PERFORMANCE TASKS
Survey Determine Compile Design Conclude Predict Create Present	Global connections and conflicts affect everyone in many ways.	**PERFORMANCE TASK I:** How do global connections affect your community? You are to survey several local businesses and organizations to determine how many of them have a global connection with another country or are connected as a consumer of the products of global or multinational companies or corporations. Determine what the connections are, how they were initiated, and why the connection was made. Compile the information from your survey, and design a graphic depiction of the relationships you have found among the local businesses and foreign companies. Include your conclusions about costs and benefits to the community and predictions about any trends you see. Report the results of your survey to a local organization such as the Rotary, Chamber of Commerce, and so on.

**QUALITY CRITERIA:
"LOOK FORS"**

- Establish a clear purpose.
- Develop an instrument for data collection.
- Identify key connections/opinions.
- Organize the collected data.
- Develop a depiction of the collected data/ideas.
- Draw conclusions.
- Identify future trends.
- Develop an organized presentation.
- Share with an appropriate identified audience.

PERFORMANCE TASK II:

As an investigative journalist, you are to survey a representative sample of local citizens to determine their opinions regarding the growing involvement of international communities in businesses and industries of the United States. Compile your information, and design a graphic depiction showing what the connections are. Draw a conclusion for the evidence you have gathered, and predict how a community vote might turn out on the question of more global involvement. Create a report, and share it with the people you interviewed.

CIVIC IDEALS AND PRACTICES

Content/Concept Standards

A central purpose of social studies is the understanding of civic ideals as a critical prerequisite to full participation in society. Students need diverse opportunities to study and practice the ideals upon which our democratic republic is based. These themes emerge through the study of history, political science, and cultural anthropology, as well as global studies, law-related education, and the humanities. Students need an introduction to related experiences through community service and participation in political activities and the democratic process to influence public policy.

What students should know how to do by the end of Grade 3

The primary student is relating his or her own experience of fairness and individual versus group rights and responsibilities to democratic ideals. The context of the classroom and the school provides immediacy, authenticity, and opportunity for identification of democratic ideals and practices. Students should be able to

1. Define key ideals of the United States' democratic form of government
2. Describe personal rights and responsibilities of citizens
3. Practice participation and classroom responsibility consistent with a democratic republic
4. Explain how citizens can influence policy decisions

What students should know how to do by the end of Grade 5

Students at this level are expanding their concepts beyond their immediate experiences. The roles and influence of key historical and contemporary figures are of interest and provide strong examples for analysis and comparison. Students should be able to

1. Demonstrate an understanding of the ideals of democratic form of government by describing their application in an authentic issue or event
2. Explain how civic action influences local, state, and national policy
3. Describe how policies and citizen behavior support or conflict with stated ideals of the republic
4. Suggest and depict how citizens can influence the common good
5. Develop a logical plan of action for participating in and influencing a current issue

What students should know how to do by the end of Grade 8

Middle-grade students are intensely interested in making a difference and in applying democratic ideals to situations they perceive to affect them. Participation in service learning opportunities and debates around local issues involve them fully when they perceive themselves as having a voice. Students should be able to

1. Describe and depict the origins of key ideals of democratic government and relate sources and examples of rights and responsibilities of individuals
2. Access and describe a variety of points of view around specific issues affecting citizens
3. Explain the citizen's role and influence in public policy decisions
4. Analyze the effectiveness and value of citizen action in relation to key issues and events
5. Propose and present solutions to current issues and cite ideals addressed by the proposal

What students should know how to do by the end of Grade 12

At this level students are recognizing and taking their place in their schools and communities in identifying needs and setting their own direction in relation to the common good. They are learning through group membership and institutional example how to participate in community service and how to have their voices heard. Students should be able to

1. Explain how a democratic form of government and its ideals continue to reflect their origins in current issues such as human dignity, equity, and the rule of law

2. Analyze public policies from the perspective of multiple points of view

3. Design and present a reasoned and justified plan to influence or achieve a goal related to an issue of local public concern

4. Participate fully in identifying, describing, analyzing, and proposing solutions to local, state, and national issues through membership in formal and informal influence groups

Social Studies:
Grade 3

CIVIC IDEALS AND PRACTICES
CONTENT/CONCEPT STANDARDS 1, 2

KEY ORGANIZING QUESTION:

What are rights and responsibilities of a citizen in a democratic form of government?

KEY COMPETENCES	KEY CONCEPTS AND CONTENT	PERFORMANCE TASKS
Interview Categorize Summarize Develop Write Display	Democratic forms of government hold certain key ideals and beliefs.	**PERFORMANCE TASK I:** What does fairness mean to you? You are to investigate what fairness means by interviewing other students about what they think. Categorize your information on a chart that has "fair" on one side and "unfair" on the other side of the chart. Summarize by developing and writing a two-paragraph definition of what *fair* means to you. Include examples from your investigation of what others think, and display your paragraphs in the hall of the school.

QUALITY CRITERIA:
"LOOK FORS"

- Clearly state your purpose.
- Prepare precise questions for your interview.
- Record responses to your questions.
- Organize the collected information into two groups (fair and unfair).
- Select the main points from interviews.
- Select important details for these points.
- Write a draft summarizing your ideas.
- Share your work with others.

PERFORMANCE TASK II:
As a community classroom citizen, you are to work with a team to investigate information about the rights and responsibilities you think each student in the classroom shares as a member of the community. Use observation and interviews to support your investigation. Together with another team, categorize your information, and develop a chart of your results. Summarize your learning by writing a definition of *right* and *responsibility*. Display your charts and paragraphs in your classroom.

Social Studies:
Grade 5

Performance
Benchmark

CIVIC IDEALS AND PRACTICES
CONTENT/CONCEPT STANDARDS 1, 2

KEY ORGANIZING QUESTIONS:

How do events and people demonstrate the ideals of democratic government? What are the skills needed to be a responsible public official?

KEY COMPETENCES	KEY CONCEPTS AND CONTENT	PERFORMANCE TASKS
Research Summarize Write Publish Distribute	Democratic ideals are demonstrated every day and through a variety of situations and issues.	**PERFORMANCE TASK I:** As a personal-interest story investigator, you are to research an example of civic ideals in practice as told by a newspaper article. Summarize the event, and rewrite the story as a personal-interest article. Include information about how all those involved felt and how they were changed as a result of their experiences. Publish your article in a class newspaper, and distribute to another classroom.

QUALITY CRITERIA:
"LOOK FORS"

• Indentify your purpose.
• Collect examples of citizens demonstrating their civic ideals.
• Select one example.
• Draft an article of the selected event/person.
• Edit for corrections and changes.
• Publish in class publication.
• Distribute to others in the school.

PERFORMANCE TASK II:
Research a famous figure in history who intervened in an issue involving democratic ideals and altered the course of the issue as a result of his or her commitment to a set of ideas. Summarize the information you collect, and rewrite the event as though it is occurring today. Publish your retelling of the event in a class book titled "Heroes of History," and distribute your book by placing it in the library or sharing it with another class.

Social Studies:
Grade 8

CIVIC IDEALS AND PRACTICES
CONTENT/CONCEPT STANDARDS 3, 4

KEY ORGANIZING QUESTION:

How can ordinary citizens influence policy decisions?

KEY COMPETENCES	KEY CONCEPTS AND CONTENT	PERFORMANCE TASKS
Collect Select Analyze Design Develop Conclude Distribute	Participation in local governmental decisions is a clear right and a responsibility of citizenship in a democracy. Participation in the governmental process influences outcomes.	**PERFORMANCE TASK I:** How does your local community government operate? For 2 weeks you are to collect newspaper articles, attend a city council meeting or committee meeting, and interview an official if possible. Select an issue that has been addressed, and analyze its development from introduction to decision. How did citizens influence the ultimate decision? Do you think ordinary citizens can influence the outcome of an issue? Design and develop a depiction of the process that also demonstrates your conclusions. Display your depiction at the city hall or other local display site.

QUALITY CRITERIA:
"LOOK FORS"

- Identify your purpose or goal.
- Gather a variety of articles and other information related to your goal.
- Clarify how individuals influenced the development of the issue.
- Design a rough draft of your ideas.
- Include your personal conclusions.
- Develop your final product.
- Distribute your final product to others in the community.

PERFORMANCE TASK II:
As an informed citizen of your school, you are to attend a meeting of your local school board and collect as much information as possible about the issues that are addressed by the board. Select an issue that is of particular interest to you, and analyze the decision that the board makes about the issue. Design and develop a newsletter that includes information about all sides of the issue, how the issue was influenced, how the decision was made about it, and your conclusions about the input of local citizens and the board members. Distribute your newsletter within your neighborhood.

Social Studies:
Grade 12

Performance
Benchmark

CIVIC IDEALS AND PRACTICES
CONTENT/CONCEPT STANDARD 1

KEY ORGANIZING QUESTION:

What do popular terms mean when they are turned into action (for example, *equity, human dignity, rule of law, access*)?

KEY COMPETENCES	KEY CONCEPTS AND CONTENT	PERFORMANCE TASKS
Investigate Collect Analyze Decide Develop Speak Present	The voice of democracy is heard when it is accompanied by congruent actions in everyday as well as in catalytic events.	**PERFORMANCE TASK I:** What does *equity and access* mean? This popular term is used in a variety of situations and settings and is a concept that has multiple meanings and interpretations. You are to investigate what a wide variety of people mean when they talk about equity and access. A good place to start would be with your teacher, your peers from a range of racial and ethnic backgrounds, as well as books and articles on the topics. Collect information from a wide range of sources. Analyze your collected data, and decide what the term means to you. Develop a speech about your conclusions. Include various examples. Present your speech to the class or to a meeting of a local community organization. **PERFORMANCE TASK II:** If you see someone's rights being violated by authorities, can you and should you intervene or do something about it? Many highly publicized reports of civil rights violations are in the news. What is the truth, and where do you stand on this issue? You are to investigate a recent example of charges of rights violations. Collect information from multiple sources and from all points of view. Analyze your collected data, and decide what you believe to be true about the reports. Develop a speech that includes the "civil rights" in the issue and your considered decision. Present your speech to another class or local organization.

QUALITY CRITERIA:
"LOOK FORS"

• Clearly define your objective.
• Gather information on your topic.
• Collect ideas and points of view of various social groups.
• Review the gathered information.
• Draw your own personal conclusions.
• Develop an oral presentation on your position.
• Present it to members of your class or an appropriate community group.

2
TECHNOLOGY CONNECTIONS

SUMMARY

Why Address Technology in a Performance-Based Curriculum?

A performance-based curriculum starts with the understanding that students will make use of what they learn in the production and dissemination of knowledge. Technology is revolutionizing the way we access information; the capabilities we have in interpreting and analyzing data; the methods by which we produce, design, and construct products resulting from our learning; the forms those products take; the methods by which the products are disseminated; and the evaluation procedures we can undertake. *Access, interpret, produce, disseminate,* and *evaluate:* These are the five central learning actions in a performance-based curriculum. These learning actions used in conjunction with technology give the learner more power and lead to greater effectiveness.

PERFORMANCE-BASED LEARNING ACTIONS WHEEL

CONTINUOUS ASSESSMENT FOR LEARNING

VARIOUS CONTEXTS - CONTENT - INFORMATION - CONCEPTS AND PERFORMING

EXTERNAL PERFORMANCE CRITERIA AND STANDARDS

ACCESSING (INVESTIGATING, GATHERING, OBSERVING, READING, INTERVIEWING)

INTERPRETING (ANALYZING, COMPARING, CONTRASTING, CATEGORIZING)

LEARNER WITH A PURPOSE, AN ISSUE, A QUESTION, OR AN IDEA

EVALUATING (REVIEWING, REVISITING, REFLECTING, COMPARING)

PRODUCING (DESIGNING, DEVELOPING, CREATING, CONSTRUCTING)

DISSEMINATING (PUBLISHING, PRESENTING, DEBATING, PERFORMING)

Technology as Content

Our physical, social, and material worlds are being radically changed as a result of the explosion of new technologies. Technological change and the issues stemming from that change provide content that is increasingly addressed in the study of history, economics, political science, and other disciplines making up the social sciences. They are also subject matter for novels, science fiction, and political and social essays. Technology is a central focus of futuristic studies. It is a product of, as well as a critical ingredient in, modern science. Technological developments have radically altered the tools used by authors and everyone involved in communication and the use of language. Technology is a rich source of topics for integrating a performance-based curriculum.

Technology as a Tool

Technology is also used as a tool in a performance-based curriculum. Although technology can be used as a way of controlling the learner's interaction with the curriculum, technology is most appropriately used as a tool controlled by the learner in the performance-based approach to learning. It is that approach that is applied in correlating this section with the Social Studies section.

Many technologies can enhance a performance-based curriculum. Their common characteristic is that they are tools that improve communication of and access to multimedia data (words, numbers, sounds, still and motion pictures, still and motion graphics) and make the use of those data easier and more effective. In a perfect world, every student and teacher would have a workstation equipped with a computer, modem, CD-ROM, laserdisc player, and a videotape camera and player. This workstation would be connected to networks that allow access to multimedia data on demand. The networks would distribute information in multimedia format to others throughout the world. In addition to these workstations, teachers and learners would have access to copying, scanning, and printing machines; CD-ROM presses; video editing equipment; audio recording and editing equipment; and software to support writing, computer-aided design, statistics, graphing, musical and artistic productions, and so on. Additional equipment would be found in a science laboratory, including tools for specialized data collection and analysis. In other specialty areas, such as art, lithographic presses would be available. Drafting equipment, electronic tools, and other specialized technologies would be present where necessary to allow the teaching of those technological subject areas.

Technology is a tool (among other tools) useful for acquiring, storing, manipulating, and communicating information in a multimedia format. Technology will be used to gather data, explore questions, produce products, and communicate results.

Technology in Support of Learning Actions

Five learning actions are central to a performance-based curriculum: **ACCESS, INTERPRET, PRODUCE, DISSEMINATE,** and **EVALUATE**. Throughout this curriculum framework, the use of appropriate technologies will support students in being active learners. Students will be encouraged to use technology to generate questions and identify problems in a wide variety of contexts; formulate hypotheses and generate tentative solutions to the questions or the problems they have defined; test the reasonableness of their answers and respond to challenges to their positions; reach a conclusion about an issue, a problem, or a question and use that "solution" as a jumping-off place to ask other questions; and engage in the learning process again.

A learner with a purpose, an issue, a question, or an idea needs to be able to use appropriate technologies in carrying out these learning actions. Technology is especially important in accessing information, producing products, and disseminating the results of one's work. We organize the benchmarks of the skills students must have in using technology around these key learning actions that can take full advantage of current technologies: **ACCESS, PRODUCE,** and **DISSEMINATE**. Examples have been developed for some strands at each of the grade levels. Each example contains suggestions on how to use technology to **ACCESS** information, **PRODUCE** products, and **DISSEMINATE** the results of one's efforts. These examples are meant to stimulate and facilitate the mastery of the use of appropriate technologies in the pursuit of learning. The suggested technologies encompass a broad range of tools useful in accessing, producing, and disseminating data that are not just words and numbers but are also sounds, still and motion graphics, and still and motion pictures. Students and teachers are encouraged to use all appropriate tools and disseminate their products using a combination of technologies.

Technology changes rapidly. The skills and abilities described below require modification on a regular basis to reflect the latest technologies. These skills and abilities must be understood as dynamic objectives rather than as static goals. They are essential learning actions that increase the student's ability to **ACCESS, PRODUCE,** and **DISSEMINATE**.

SKILLS AND ABILITIES

How students should be able to use technology by the end of Grade 3

Access:

A1	Gather information with still, digital, or video camera
A2	Search databases to locate information
A3	Gather sounds and conversations with audio and video recorders
A4	Collect digitized audio data
A5	Access information on laserdisc by using bar code reader
A6	Scan to capture graphic data
A7	Copy to gather graphics
A8	Retrieve and print information using a computer
A9	Gather information through telephone
A10	Select and use information from CDs
A11	Fax to send and receive printed information
A12	Identify and use all types of materials, such as print, nonprint, and electronic media
A13	Locate information using electronic indexes or media

Produce:

P1	Draw and paint graphics and pictures using a computer
P2	Create flip card animations using a computer
P3	Design and develop computer products including pictures, text, flip card animations, sounds, and graphics
P4	Design and develop audiotapes
P5	Design and develop videotapes
P6	Create overhead or slide presentations with or without background music
P7	Develop stories using computer-generated text with either handmade or computer-generated illustrations

Disseminate:

D1	Present *Logo* or *HyperCard* (or similar) computer product including pictures, text, flip card animations, sounds, and graphics
D2	Publish printed page including text and graphics
D3	Broadcast audiotape
D4	Broadcast videotape
D5	Present overhead or slide presentation
D6	Fax information to other audiences
D7	Explain products or creations to an audience

How students should be able to use technology by the end of Grade 5

Access:

A1   Gather information with a still, digital, or video camera of moderate complexity

A2   Gather information using text-based databases to locate information

A3   Access information on laserdisc by using bar code reader and computer controls

A4   Gather information using telephone and modem to connect to other users and databases (Internet, eWorld, etc.)

A5   Search basic library technologies for data

A6   Select and use specialized tools appropriate to grade level and subject matter

A7   Record interviews with experts

A8   Scan CD collections for needed information

Produce:

P1   Create path-based animations using computer

P2   Create with computer painting and drawing tools of moderate complexity

P3   Digitize still and motion pictures

P4   Create basic spreadsheet for addition, subtraction, multiplication, and division

P5   Graph data (pie charts, line and bar graphs) using computer

P6   Create edited videotapes of moderate complexity using a videotape editing deck or computer-based digital editing system or two connected cassette recorders (VCRs)

P7   Input text into computer using keyboard with appropriate keyboard skills

P8   Design and develop moderately complex *Logo* or *HyperCard* (or similar) programs including pictures, sounds, flip card and path-based animations, graphics, text, and motion pictures

P9   Design and develop multipage document including text and graphics using computer

P10   Create edited audiotape

P11   Create edited videotape

P12   Create overhead or slide presentation with synchronized voice narration with or without background music

P13   Lay out advertisements, posters, and banners

Disseminate:

D1   Present moderately complex *Logo* or *HyperCard* (or similar) computer product including pictures, sounds, flip card and path-based animations, graphics, text, and motion pictures

D2   Publish multipage printed document including formatted, paginated text and graphics

D3   Broadcast edited audiotape and videotape

D4   Present programs using overhead projector, slide projector, or computer

D5   Present information over public address system in a school, community, or meeting situation

D6   Display information in a variety of formats

D7   Advertise for events, services, or products

D8   Broadcast performances and products

D9   Broadcast on cable TV

How students should be able to use technology by the end of Grade 8

Access:

A1 Gather information using computer, CD-ROM, and laserdisc databases

A2 Gather data using telephone and modem (including graphics and sounds) to and from other users and databases (Internet, eWorld, etc.)

A3 Search basic spreadsheet and databasing software for "what if?" comparisons and analyses

A4 Search technologies for accessing data outside the school and local library

A5 Search menus to locate information on computer software, CD-ROM, or laserdiscs

A6 Video interviews

A7 Download information from Internet

Produce:

P1 Create products using computer painting and drawing tools, including moderately complex color tools

P2 Digitize still and motion pictures

P3 Create edited videotapes by using a videotape editing deck or computer-based digital editing system

P4 Create computer presentation program

P5 Develop cell-based animations using computer

P6 Design and develop complex *Logo* or *HyperCard* (or similar) programs including still pictures; flip card, path-based, and cell-based animations; sounds; graphics; and motion pictures

P7 Create multipage documents including text and graphics using computer page layout tools

P8 Develop audiotapes that combine sounds and voice data from a variety of sources

P9 Produce videotapes that are organized, coherent, and well edited

P10 Create a personal database requiring the collection of data over time

Disseminate:

D1 Present relatively complex *Logo* or *HyperCard* (or similar) product including still pictures; flip card, path-based, and cell-based animations; sounds; graphics; and motion pictures

D2 Publish multipage printed documents including text and graphics

D3 Broadcast edited audiotape of moderate complexity

D4 Broadcast edited videotape of moderate complexity

D5 Broadcast video presentation over schoolwide Channel 1 (Whittle), citywide public Channel 28, or citywide ITFS schools-only equipment

D6 Advertise events, services, or products

D7 Display information and designs on various formats available

D8 Broadcast on closed circuit or cable television

D9 Broadcast filmed and live performances on television

D10 Distribute over available sources in Internet

How students should be able to use technology by the end of Grade 12

Access:

A1   Access and use complex electronic databases and communication networks of all types including, but not limited to, Internet

A2   Research using sensors, probes, and other specialized scientific tools as appropriate

A3   Gather information from spreadsheet, databasing software, and statistical packages, including the use of formulas and charting routines

A4   Search technologies for data and primary sources (publications and persons)

A5   Identify local, regional, and national databases and procedures for needed data

A6   Review online bulletin boards, databases, and electronic retrieval services for data

Produce:

P1   Create with complex computer painting and drawing tools and programs

P2   Create 3-D graphics using drawing and modeling tools

P3   Create changing images using computer digital-morphing programs

P4   Illustrate concrete and abstract concepts using computer-aided design and mathematical modeling

P5   Create CD-ROM simulations

P6   Create complex cell-based animations, including 3-D objects, using the computer

P7   Create complex *Logo* or *HyperCard* (or similar) programs including pictures; flip card, path-based, and cell-based animations; sounds; 3-D graphics; and motion pictures

P8   Develop multipage documents with information from a variety of sources, including text and graphics using appropriate computer page layout tools

P9   Create documents using a variety of fonts and type faces

P10   Assemble findings based on spreadsheets, databasing software, and statistical packages involving the use of formulas as appropriate

P11   Design graphic and text titles for digital video productions

P12   Develop digitally edited materials including audio, motion pictures, still-frame pictures, motion graphics, and still-frame graphics

P13   Design and develop a personal database of moderate complexity

P14   Illustrate concrete and abstract mathematical and scientific concepts

P15   Assemble information by creating, searching, and sorting databases

P16   Design and develop a dissemination design for video using ITFS microwave and satellite up-and-down links

Disseminate:

D1   Transmit complex *Logo* or *HyperCard* (or similar) computer product including pictures; flip card, path-based, and cell-based animations; sounds; 3-D graphics; and motion pictures

D2   Publish multipage printed documents, appropriately laid out, including text and graphics

D3   Transmit complex spreadsheet or database findings

D4   Telecast digital video product of some complexity

D5   Present computer-based animation program (cell- or path-based animations, or both)

D6   Publish reports generated from database searches

D7   Publish scientific investigations and results or recommendations

D8   Transmit a video presentation to secondary students using ITFS microwave, Whittle Channel 1 equipment, public Channel 28, cable hookups, and satellite up-and-down links to local schools or students in other school systems

D9   Share product or presentation with a panel of experts

Technology Connections
Social Studies: Grade 3

CULTURE
CORRESPONDING PERFORMANCE BENCHMARK, PAGE 18

KEY ORGANIZING QUESTION:

How are individuals and groups alike and different?

ACCESS	PRODUCE	DISSEMINATE
PERFORMANCE TASK I: You are to investigate the influences of weather and geography on people in particular regions. Use a digital database, a CD-ROM, or the Internet to locate pictures or art that identify various types of dress, homes, work, food, or leisure activities one might find in various regions of the United States. Analyze the unique details of the pictures you collect.	**PERFORMANCE TASK I:** Copy the pictures into a paint or drawing program, a word processing program, or hypercard. Use this information to create a poster to show how weather and/or geography might be reasons for these differences.	**PERFORMANCE TASK I:** Print your product, or use the computer to present your creation to a group of students in your class.
PERFORMANCE TASK II: As an investigative reporter, collect information on the origin of some of the last names of students in your class. Use a digital database, a CD-ROM, or the Internet to gather your information. Analyze the collected data by categorizing it.	**PERFORMANCE TASK II:** Copy the collected data into a drawing or paint program, word processing program, or hypercard. Use this information to create a poster showing the origin of two different family names.	**PERFORMANCE TASK II:** Print your product, or use the computer to present your product and explanation to a group of students in your class.

Technology Connections
Social Studies: Grade 5

**Performance
Benchmark**

CULTURE
CORRESPONDING PERFORMANCE BENCHMARK, PAGE 19

KEY ORGANIZING QUESTION:

How do people interpret their experiences based on their cultural perspectives and frames of reference?

ACCESS	PRODUCE	DISSEMINATE
PERFORMANCE TASK I: You are to gather information about the United States and a selected foreign country. Include information related to beliefs, religion, food, homes, government, geography, clothing, and family life. You can get this information from CD-ROMs or from the Internet. Paste your gathered information into your paint and draw program, or your word processing program.	**PERFORMANCE TASK I:** Create pages or slides that best depict a topic and show the differences between the United States and your selected country. Use a program like Power Point to create your slides.	**PERFORMANCE TASK I:** Present your computer presentation to another class. Donate your slide show to the class library where it could serve as a resource in future classes.
PERFORMANCE TASK II: As a cultural investigator, use the computer to research how people in a culture use stories, music, and folktales to tell others about their culture. Use a CD-ROM or the Internet to find examples or evidence.	**PERFORMANCE TASK II:** Summarize the collected information, and create a written report on your word processing program. Be sure to include visuals to support your report.	**PERFORMANCE TASK II:** Print out your report, and publish it in a booklet form. Present your findings and your conclusions to a group of students from another class.

Technology Connections
Social Studies: Grade 8

CULTURE
CORRESPONDING PERFORMANCE BENCHMARK, PAGE 20

KEY ORGANIZING QUESTION:

How do differences within various aspects of culture contribute to conflict across cultures?

ACCESS	PRODUCE	DISSEMINATE
PERFORMANCE TASK I: As an investigative reporter, select a current event or topic on which two cultures or two groups are in conflict. Gather information on the history, the initial cause, and the development of the event. Gather information on both sides of the issues.	**PERFORMANCE TASK I:** Design and develop a video that portrays the event or topic and the two conflicting viewpoints. Include a personal summary of the situation and a recommendation for resolving the conflict.	**PERFORMANCE TASK I:** Present your video to a seventh-grade social studies class. Ask them to reflect on the message in your video, and see if they can offer recommendations for resolving the conflict.
PERFORMANCE TASK II: As an investigative reporter, select one aspect of a culture (e.g., values, religion, dress, drama, art, family life, music, etc.), and investigate how this one aspect is demonstrated in three different cultures. Take pictures if possible with a digitized camera capturing examples of your cultural aspect, or use a regular camera and scan the pictures into a program.	**PERFORMANCE TASK II:** Analyze how the differences could create conlict across cultures. Using your computer program, create a visual depiction using your pictures and a written description of how these differences could create conflict across cultures.	**PERFORMANCE TASK II:** Print out a hard copy of your depiction and a written explanation on the different ways cultures respond to your selected cultural aspect. Present your publication and information to a group of students from another class.

Technology Connections
Social Studies: Grade 12

Performance Benchmark

CULTURE
CORRESPONDING PERFORMANCE BENCHMARK, PAGE 21

KEY ORGANIZING QUESTION:

How does discrimination affect cultural survival, then and now?

ACCESS	PRODUCE	DISSEMINATE
PERFORMANCE TASK I: Interview people from three different cultures within your school or your community. Find out in what ways they may have experienced discrimination, how they felt, how they reacted, and how their culture influences their response to discrimination.	**PERFORMANCE TASK I:** Organize all of your data on a spreadsheet. Analyze the collected data, and draw conclusions about how cultures protect themselves from outside discrimination. Summarize your conclusions in a multimedia presentation.	**PERFORMANCE TASK I:** Present and discuss your presentation with a selected audience from the community.
PERFORMANCE TASK II: As a member of an interview team, engage a strong sampling of students or community members to learn about cultural conflicts and what the causes might be for these differences.	**PERFORMANCE TASK II:** Organize your collected data on a spreadsheet. Analyze the collected data, and write several articles on the information conveying different points of view.	**PERFORMANCE TASK II:** Publish your articles in your own cultural newsletter. Share your newsletter with a mixed group of students or community members, and lead a discussion on the main points.

Technology Connections
Social Studies: Grade 3

TIME, CONTINUITY, AND CHANGE
CORRESPONDING PERFORMANCE BENCHMARK, PAGE 24

KEY ORGANIZING QUESTION:
How can we describe how people are changed by time and events?

ACCESS	PRODUCE	DISSEMINATE
PERFORMANCE TASK I: As a historical investigator, select a senior citizen in your family or neighborhood to interview. Find out the date of their birth, and what was happening in society and the world during their early years. Ask questions about the key events they remember. Ask about the approximate dates. Ask how these events affected them as youngsters and as adults.	**PERFORMANCE TASK I:** Use the computer to create a timeline of your important citizen's life. Be sure to include all important dates and events. If they had photographs for you to use, scan them into your timeline. Write a story about this person's life. Explain what you learned about the key events and how they affected this person.	**PERFORMANCE TASK I:** Publish your timeline and your story. Invite your senior citizens to school. In groups of six—three students and three seniors—present your timelines and read your stories. Display your timelines and stories for others to see and read.
PERFORMANCE TASK II: As a historical investigator, select an event in history that affected a number of people. Explain how people who lived in the area were affected by the event.	**PERFORMANCE TASK II:** Construct a visual depiction of the event using a paint and draw program on the computer. Type a story on the computer explaining how people experienced the event and how they were affected by it. Tell what you think they learned from the event and how they felt.	**PERFORMANCE TASK II:** Read your story to a group of students from another class. Share your computer-generated depiction. Ask for their reactions.

**Technology Connections
Social Studies: Grade 5**

**Performance
Benchmark**

TIME, CONTINUITY, AND CHANGE
CORRESPONDING PERFORMANCE BENCHMARK, PAGE 25

KEY ORGANIZING QUESTION:

How do people interpret the same events differently?

ACCESS	PRODUCE	DISSEMINATE
PERFORMANCE TASK I: As a newswriter, choose a current event, and research the facts and accounts of the event from a variety of sources. Be sure to use a reputable mix from the Internet.	**PERFORMANCE TASK I:** Compare and contrast the various accounts of the event. Using a table and graph or draw program, create a storyboard of the event concentrating on the information that is consistent across your sources. Write your own account of the event using a word processing program.	**PERFORMANCE TASK I:** Present copies of your story-board and written account to an audience of students from another class. Be sure to explain how easy it is for people to interpret the same event differently. Ask for their reflections and ideas.
PERFORMANCE TASK II: As a writer, choose a current event and research the facts and accounts of the event from a variety of sources including many from the Internet and CD-ROM.	**PERFORMANCE TASK II:** Compare and contrast accounts of the event. Identify the key aspects of the event. Using a word processing program, write a draft of the event as though it happened 100 years ago. Be sure to import or scan illustrations into your final document.	**PERFORMANCE TASK II:** Run copies of your written and illustrated account. Present your ideas to students from a history class or your school. Share copies of your written account, and be sure to explain how the event could be misinterpreted based on the passage of time and changing events.

Technology Connections
Social Studies: Grade 8

Performance
Benchmark

TIME, CONTINUITY, AND CHANGE
CORRESPONDING PERFORMANCE BENCHMARK, PAGE 26

KEY ORGANIZING QUESTION:

How is history both documented and "altered" based on a combination of fact, opinion, bias, and point of view?

ACCESS	PRODUCE	DISSEMINATE
PERFORMANCE TASK I: Is it possible for different types of media to convey a particular slant or point of view? Collect information about a current event from an extensive range of media texts.	**PERFORMANCE TASK I:** Analyze the various text types for the perspective presented. How was meaning implied in the message? How did you respond to the message? How do others respond or react? How does the technique influence or impact the message? Select a political or social topic of interest, then design and develop a slide-tape presentation or a video on the topic integrating forms and techniques creatively so it will motivate a particular response from your audience (e.g., starving children in a Third World country).	**PERFORMANCE TASK I:** Share your presentation with a panel of historians and psychologists. Ask them for their personal feelings and reactions to your message, the form of your message, and the special techniques you employed. Evaluate your presentation based on the effectiveness of the product to communicate a particular point of view and/or to elicit a particular emotional response. How can this type of communicating affect the documentation of history?
PERFORMANCE TASK II: As a historical investigator, collect examples of current and historical political cartoons. Use a range of media texts to create your collection.	**PERFORMANCE TASK II:** Analyze your collection by categorizing and labeling the symbols and images the cartoonists used to influence the point of view and opinions of the viewers. For example, animals such as skunks have been used to portray crooked politicians. Use a computer program to create a chart or graph of the various symbols, images, and emotional responses possible from your cartoon collection. Scan your cartoons into a computer program, and create a slide presentation.	**PERFORMANCE TASK II:** Present your cartoons to a government class. Ask them to respond on a response sheet to each cartoon by recording their reactions to the various symbols, images, and intended messages. Following your presentation, analyze their responses to determine how history is documented and altered based on a combination of fact, opinion, bias, and point of view.

Technology Connections
Social Studies: Grade 12

Performance
Benchmark

TIME, CONTINUITY, AND CHANGE
CORRESPONDING PERFORMANCE BENCHMARK, PAGE 27

KEY ORGANIZING QUESTION:

What are examples of patterns in history, and why are they repeated over time?

ACCESS	PRODUCE	DISSEMINATE
PERFORMANCE TASK I: As a researcher, select a concept that presents itself in history such as war, revolution, crime, or hunger. Gather information, examples, and patterns from history on this topic. Also collect examples of the way your concept is projected through various works of literature. Analyze the events, and summarize your own conclusions about the patterns in history and why they are repeated over time.	**PERFORMANCE TASK I:** Design and develop a multimedia presentation that clearly depicts your findings in a unique and creative manner. Be sure to include appropriate background music for your message or messages.	**PERFORMANCE TASK I:** Deliver your presentation to an eighth-grade social studies class. Be prepared with open-ended questions to lead a discussion on the ideas presented and the reactions evoked. Record the discussion, and analyze it later to see if your production successfully conveyed your intended message.
PERFORMANCE TASK II: As a researcher, select two countries in which there has been a history of rapid political change. Use technology to gather as much information as possible. Analyze your gathered information, and then compare these two countries for similar events, issues, leadership, or perseverance, and cultural background that influenced the changes.	**PERFORMANCE TASK II:** Design and develop a multimedia production that clearly depicts your findings and conclusions in a unique and creative manner. Be sure to include and use music appropriately to convey your message.	**PERFORMANCE TASK II:** Deliver your presentation to an eighth-grade social studies class. Prepare a series of open-ended questions on the ideas in your multimedia production to lead a discussion following your presentation. Record the discussion, and analyze it later to see if your production successfully conveyed your intended message.

3
PERFORMANCE DESIGNERS

The ultimate key to success with performance-based education is the creativity, rigor, and consistency of focus that must characterize the ongoing instructional process in the classroom. Student success with the performance benchmarks identified in this text depends on daily interactions with the learning actions. Students must feel empowered to demonstrate the learning actions being taught so they can internalize them, take ownership, and apply them easily in the benchmark performances. They must be able to do this through a continuous improvement process with a focus on quality criteria.

In order to accomplish the performance benchmarks in this text, learners must have daily practice with the routine of learning and demonstrating through learning actions as they gain new understanding about concepts from the different disciplines. They must recognize that only through continuous improvement will they achieve the defined quality that must be their goal.

If this is to occur, teachers must design lessons specifically addressing the learning actions (access, interpret, produce, disseminate, and evaluate). Instruction on these learning actions will engage students in gathering and interpreting information so they can produce a product, service, or performance with their newly acquired insights and knowledge. Then they can disseminate or give their product, service, or performance to an authentic audience. They do all of these learning actions with a continuous focus on evaluating themselves and their work against the identified quality criteria that the teacher will be looking for.

The performance designer is a tool for teachers to use when planning for students to engage in a significant demonstration that is an interactive experience for students designed to include essential content, competence (learning actions), context (issue, situation, and audience), and quality criteria.

The completed performance designer will describe the total performance or demonstration of significance. All of the students' actions will be clearly stated. The teacher uses this performance designer to develop the necessary instructional sequences that will support the attainment of each of the desired actions. Once students know how to do the actions, they are ready to pursue the planned performance.

The following organizer provides an overview. Each major section in the planner is identified and corresponds to a detailed explanation that follows.

PERFORMANCE DESIGNER FORMAT

I	**Ⓐ PURPOSE**	What complex thinking process is the focus?
	Ⓑ KEY ORGANIZING QUESTION	An issue or challenge to investigate.
	Ⓒ ROLE	You are _____ who is expected to ...

	(Do what?)	*(With what?)*	*(How well?)*
II	**Ⓓ** Access and **Ⓔ** interpret by...	**Ⓕ** CONTENT/CONCEPTS	**Ⓖ** QUALITY CRITERIA "Look fors"

	(In order to...	*...do what?)*	*(How well?)*
III	**Ⓗ** Produce by...	**Ⓘ** PRODUCT/ PERFORMANCE	**Ⓙ** QUALITY CRITERIA "Look fors"

		(To/for whom? Where?)	*(How well?)*
IV	**Ⓚ** Disseminate by...	**Ⓛ** AUDIENCE/ SETTING	**Ⓜ** QUALITY CRITERIA "Look fors"

Section I

The first section of the designer serves as an organizer for the key elements that follow.

PERFORMANCE DESIGNER ELEMENT	REFLECTIVE QUESTIONS
Ⓐ PURPOSE The reason the performance is worth doing. This section may be tied to state- or district-level assessment. It will more often relate to a complex thinking process that is the result of applied critical-reasoning skills. (Example: drawing a conclusion, making a recommendation)	What do I want to be sure students are more competent doing when this performance is complete? Do I want them to be able to develop a range of possible solutions to a problem? Will they investigate an issue from outside school, form an opinion, or describe and support a point of view? What complex thinking skill is the core purpose of this performance?
Ⓑ KEY ORGANIZING QUESTION As with the purpose, the question focuses and organizes the entire performance. It combines with the role and the audience to define the context.	What will the students be accessing information about? Do I want to select the issue or question to be accessed, or will the students determine the learning they will pursue? Is the question or issue developmentally appropriate, and can I facilitate obtaining the resources that students will need for the issue? Do the students have any experiential background for this issue? Will the experience be limited to learning from the experiences of others?
Ⓒ ROLE When students take on a role, the point of view of the role adds a dimension not common to most learning. The role introduces the prompt that initiates the entire performance.	Will this role be authentic? Or is it a role-play? For example, students as artists, authors, and investigators are real roles for students. Students as lawyers, policemen, or city council members do not have the same level of authenticity. They would be role-playing, which is pretending to be someone. Will there be more than one role, or will students all be in the same role? How will I ensure that students will have a focused point of view to explore? In life outside school, who would answer this question or be concerned with this issue? What would that expert do? Who is the expert? What's the real role?

Section II

The second section of the performance designer focuses on having students carry out the learning actions of accessing and interpreting necessary content and concepts. The right-hand column of the top section defines the quality criteria, or "look fors," that will be taught, practiced, and assessed. These are the quality criteria of the performance benchmarks.

PERFORMANCE DESIGNER ELEMENT	REFLECTIVE QUESTIONS
❶ ACCESS AND Accessing actions might require students to interview, locate, or read for information. The importance of student involvement in acquiring information requires a shift from teacher as information provider to teacher as facilitator for information accessing.	Where can information be accessed? Are there experts who can be interviewed? What publications will be helpful? Which texts contain related information? Who can we contact on the Internet? What other resources are available?
❷ INTERPRET BY... *(Do what?)* Interpreting actions requires students to review what they have collected and decide what it means now that they have it. Students may categorize the information they have, compare it with what they already know, and process it in a variety of critical and creative ways.	How will students interact with the information they have collected? Will they formulate new questions? Will they begin to be asked to draw conclusions or perhaps make predictions at this point in the performance? Who will students interact with to communicate their initial interpretations of the information? Will they have a peer conference? Will I ask questions or give answers?
❸ CONTENT/CONCEPTS *(With what?)* This specifies the knowledge or information the students are to learn. The result at the end is only going to be as good as the information the students collect. The resources should go far beyond the text. The teacher should support with additional resources and literature examples.	What do the students need to know? Where will the information come from? What will be significant learning to retain after the performance is over? Why is it important for students to learn this? Where might they need to use it later? Next year? After they leave school? What connections can they make to other knowledge structures? What are different points of view?
❹ QUALITY CRITERIA **("Look fors")** *(How well?)* Quality criteria are the specifications for the performance. It is critical that these "look fors" be observable and measurable and that they represent high-quality performances. The quality criteria stated in the third column will integrate the learning actions in the left-hand column with the content/concept to be learned in the center column.	What would an expert interviewer or artist do? What would be observable in the performance of a quality questioner or researcher? How would I know one if I saw one? Do the criteria match the learning action that has been selected, and do they describe a logical and relevant application of the content/concept that is to be learned?

Section III

The third main section on the performance designer is organized similarly but focuses on the producing action or competence in the Learning Actions Wheel. The middle column of this section allows the teacher to describe or specify the nature of the product or performance the students are to generate. The right-hand column describes the quality criteria, or "look fors," that pertain to that product or production.

PERFORMANCE DESIGNER ELEMENT	REFLECTIVE QUESTIONS
❽ PRODUCE BY... *(In order to...* Producing actions ask students to synthesize their learning, to bring what has been learned together into a cohesive whole that has relevance. Students might design, build, develop, create, construct, or illustrate.	How will students bring what they have learned together? What actions will lead to a product and keep the students in the role? Are there stages to the producing action, such as design and develop or draft and write? What are the essential actions that will lead to a product?
❾ PRODUCT/PERFORMANCE *...do what?)* This describes the product, service, or production that the student will address. It should be something that will benefit the authentic audience.	What would an expert create? How does this product relate to the required or identified knowledge base? How does this product incorporate the required skills? What impact should the product have on the audience?
❿ QUALITY CRITERIA **("Look fors")** *(How well?)* Quality criteria describe the learning actions as they occur in conjunction with the development of the product, service, or production. It is critical that the criteria be observable, and measurable, and that it represent quality.	What would an excellent product look like? How could it be described? Will the product or production indicate the designing and developing that were used? How can it be precisely described in relationship to the learning actions? What are the essential actions the student will perform that relate to the producing verbs?

Section IV

The last section of the performance designer relates to the disseminating learning actions. It describes the sharing of the product. The middle column of this section clearly denotes the *audience* and the *setting*, or *context*, in which the performance will occur. These factors are critical in determining the realistic impact of the student's learning. The right-hand column will describe the quality criteria for this portion of the performance designer by combining the disseminating action in relationship with the authentic audience. It defines the purpose for the learning.

PERFORMANCE DESIGNER ELEMENT	REFLECTIVE QUESTIONS
Ⓚ DISSEMINATE BY... Learning actions at this stage of the role performance or demonstration have the learners presenting their products, services, or productions. The form of the presentation will vary depending on the original purpose. The learner might disseminate by explaining, teaching, or dancing.	What will be the most efficient and effective form of communicating this new product? Will students choose to broadcast or publish or teach? How does this form best relate to the product and the purpose? How does this delivery relate to the role?
Ⓛ AUDIENCE/SETTING **(To/for whom? Where?)** The audience is the recipient of the learners' product or production. The degree of authenticity will be reflected in the composition of the audience. The setting for this performance could be related to the original issue being investigated as well as the purpose for this investigation, or the natural location of the recipient.	Who will benefit from the students' learning? Who can use this recommendation or this finding? Is it another learner? Someone at another grade level? Is it a team of engineers at General Motors? Or young patients in a dentist's office? Where is the audience?
Ⓜ QUALITY CRITERIA **("Look fors")** **(How well?)** The criteria describe the specification for delivering the product, service, or performance. They are observable and represent quality.	What does a quality presentation look like? What are the essential elements that clearly define a quality presentation? How do the criteria connect the disseminating actions with the learner and the audience?

The performance designer gives teachers a very useful tool for continuously defining learning in terms of a realistic role that students must either individually or collectively take on and accomplish. The performance designer also continuously engages students in the range of learning actions that successful people engage in after they graduate from school, but it does so in the safe environment of school under the careful guidance of the teacher. Learners will demonstrate each role performance according to their developmental level of growth. Continuous involvement and experience with learning actions and quality criteria will result in demonstrated student improvement and continuous upleveling of quality criteria that will fully prepare students for any performance benchmark they are asked to demonstrate.

EXAMPLES OF LEARNING ACTIONS

ACCESS:
Investigate
Gather
Interview
Research
Listen
Observe
Collect
Search
Inquire
Survey
View
Discover
Read
Explore
Examine

INTERPRET:
Analyze
Explain
Paraphrase
Rephrase
Clarify
Compare
Contrast
Summarize
Integrate
Evaluate
Translate
Prioritize
Synthesize
Sort
Classify

PRODUCE:
Create
Design
Develop
Draw
Write
Lay out
Build
Draft
Invent
Erect
Sketch
Assemble
Compose
Illustrate
Generate

DISSEMINATE:
Publish
Perform
Teach
Present
Transmit
Display
Explain
Broadcast
Act
Advertise
Discuss
Send
Sing
Dance
Telecast

EVALUATE:
Review
Reflect
Assess
Revisit
Compare
Conclude
Generalize
Prove
Question
Refute
Support
Verify
Test
Realign
Judge

SAMPLE PERFORMANCE DESIGNER FOR GRADE 3

PURPOSE:
To make wise choices

SOCIAL STUDIES:
PRODUCTION, DISTRIBUTION, AND CONSUMPTION
(SEE PAGE 54)

- -

KEY ORGANIZING QUESTION:
How can we distinguish between needs and wants when we make choices for consumption?

- -

ROLE: *(You are ...)*
A clever consumer

(Who is expected to ...)

COMPETENCE (Do what?)	CONTENT/CONCEPTS (With what?)	QUALITY CRITERIA ("Look fors")
Access and interpret by ... gathering and analyzing	information from a variety of resources on a popular food product that is considered unhealthy the collected information to learn why it's popular, why it's unhealthy, and why sales are so good.	• Identify your task. • Decide where to get materials and information. • Collect information from a variety of resources. • Identify the major points. • Select the most important ideas. • Organize the ideas into specific categories.

COMPETENCE (In order to ...	PRODUCT/PERFORMANCE ... do what?)	QUALITY CRITERIA ("Look fors")
Produce by ... designing and developing	a chart or table to show your collected information. Be sure to include examples of advertisements, costs, and responses from consumers.	• Identify your audience. • Include accurate details. • Create a draft. • Check for impact and accuracy. • Create a finished product.

COMPETENCE	AUDIENCE / SETTING (To/for whom? Where?)	QUALITY CRITERIA ("Look fors")
Disseminate by ... presenting and explaining	your chart to students in another class and/or the school nurse or dietician.	• Select appropriate method for presenting. • Organize your ideas and your message. • Include important details. • Share your conclusion. • Ask for reactions.

SAMPLE PERFORMANCE DESIGNER FOR GRADE 5

PURPOSE:

To reach a conclusion

SOCIAL STUDIES:
PEOPLE, PLACES, AND ENVIRONMENTS
(SEE PAGE 31)

- -

KEY ORGANIZING QUESTION:

How do landforms, weather, and geographic features affect where people live and work?

- -

ROLE: *(You are ...)*

An environmental investigator

(Who is expected to ...)

COMPETENCE *(Do what?)*	CONTENT/CONCEPTS *(With what?)*	QUALITY CRITERIA *("Look fors")*

Access and interpret by ...
 	
   investigating
 	
   and summarizing
	a state in the United States to determine the desirable resources, physical attractions, and weather conditions
	
	the various advantages your state offers to residents.
		• Identify your purpose.
		• Clearly state three to five questions you will explore.
		• Use a variety of resources.
		• Organize information into major categories.
		• Condense the information.

COMPETENCE *(In order to ...*	PRODUCT/PERFORMANCE *... do what?)*	QUALITY CRITERIA *("Look fors")*

Produce by ...
 	
   illustrating
 	
   and planning
	a mural on your state that contains all of the major advantages that would attract new residents and investors to the state
	
	a lesson on your findings.
		• Review your purpose.
		• Brainstorm key sections for the mural.
		• Create a planning sketch.
		• Check for all important details.
		• Gather necessary materials.
		• Create the final product.

COMPETENCE	AUDIENCE / SETTING *(To/for whom? Where?)*	QUALITY CRITERIA *("Look fors")*
Disseminate by ... teaching	your lesson to a group of students from the fourth grade.	• Ask audience what they know about your state. • Provide identifying information. • Use the mural as a visual teaching tool. • Summarize your main ideas. • Ask if they think people would find your state appealing.

SAMPLE PERFORMANCE DESIGNER FOR GRADE 8

PURPOSE:
To summarize and make connections

SOCIAL STUDIES:
SCIENCE, TECHNOLOGY, AND SOCIETY
(SEE PAGE 62)

KEY ORGANIZING QUESTION:
How can decisions be made about control of the development and use of scientific advancements?

ROLE: *(You are ...)*
A student teacher

(Who is expected to ...)

COMPETENCE (*Do what?*)	CONTENT/CONCEPTS (*With what?*)	QUALITY CRITERIA (*"Look fors"*)

Access and interpret by ...
 	
    researching
 	
    and summarizing
	a technological advancement and its potential for positive or negative impact on society
	
	your findings on the particular technological advancement.
		• Identify your purpose.
		• Identify reputable resources.
		• Select detailed information.
		• Select the main points.
		• Provide important details.
		• Condense the message.

COMPETENCE (*In order to ...*	PRODUCT/PERFORMANCE *... do what?*)	QUALITY CRITERIA (*"Look fors"*)

Produce by ...
    designing
 	
    and predicting
	a lesson on your findings
	
	possible future applications or outgrowths.
		• Restate your purpose.
		• Create an outline for your lesson.
		• Create needed visuals.
		• Review and edit as necessary.
		• State predictions.

COMPETENCE	AUDIENCE / SETTING (*To/for whom? Where?*)	QUALITY CRITERIA (*"Look fors"*)
Disseminate by ... teaching	a lesson on your findings to a group of sixth- or seventh-grade students.	• Engage the students with questions on your lesson. • Listen to response. • Coordinate your delivery with their responses. • Review main points. • Check for understanding.

SAMPLE PERFORMANCE DESIGNER FOR GRADE 12

PURPOSE:
To draw a conclusion

KEY ORGANIZING QUESTION:
What are the relationships between people and their environments and the effects on culture, dress, food, customs, and values?

ROLE: *(You are ...)*
A speech writer

(Who is expected to ...)

COMPETENCE (*Do what?*)	CONTENT/CONCEPTS (*With what?*)	QUALITY CRITERIA (*"Look fors"*)
Access and interpret by ... researching and explaining	the relationships between a selected people and their environment the effects of these relationships on their culture, dress, food, customs, and values.	• Identify your purpose. • Use a variety of reputable resources. • Organize information according to purpose. • Include specific, accurate details and examples.

COMPETENCE (*In order to ...*	PRODUCT/PERFORMANCE (*... do what?*)	QUALITY CRITERIA (*"Look fors"*)
Produce by ... drafting and writing	a speech on your conclusions.	• Create preliminary script. • Review message and reactions. • Edit as necessary. • State main ideas. • Support with sufficient details. • Tie conclusion to original purpose.

COMPETENCE	AUDIENCE / SETTING (*To/for whom? Where?*)	QUALITY CRITERIA (*"Look fors"*)
Disseminate by ... presenting and broadcasting	your speech for a video taping the taped speech to 10th-grade social studies classes.	• Identify your purpose for your audience. • Use standard conventions of speech for your taping. • Review audience reactions. • Compare reactions to your purpose.

SAMPLE PERFORMANCE DESIGNER FOR GRADE 3

PURPOSE:
To form an opinion

SOCIAL STUDIES:
INDIVIDUAL DEVELOPMENT AND IDENTITY
(SEE PAGE 36)

KEY ORGANIZING QUESTION:
What are the characteristics that can describe one's family history and its effects on your life today?

ROLE: *(You are ...)*
A health inspector

(Who is expected to ...)

COMPETENCE (Do what?)	CONTENT/CONCEPTS (With what?)	QUALITY CRITERIA ("Look fors")
Access and interpret by ... interviewing and summarizing	members of your family about their health histories your findings.	• State your purpose. • Write out your questions. • Record your information. • Select the main ideas. • Provide interesting and factual articles.

COMPETENCE (In order to ...)	PRODUCT/PERFORMANCE (... do what?)	QUALITY CRITERIA ("Look fors")
Produce by ... designing and writing	a health brochure on your family's health a health history and what it means to you.	• Create a draft of your brochure. • Include colorful, interesting visuals. • Review and improve as necessary. • Create your final product.

COMPETENCE	AUDIENCE / SETTING (To/for whom? Where?)	QUALITY CRITERIA ("Look fors")
Disseminate by ... publishing	your brochure for members of your family.	• Develop copies of your brochure. • Distribute to family members. • Seek their reactions.

SAMPLE PERFORMANCE DESIGNER FOR GRADE 5

PURPOSE:
To make recommendation

SOCIAL STUDIES:
INDIVIDUALS, GROUPS, AND INSTITUTIONS
(SEE PAGE 43)

KEY ORGANIZING QUESTION:
How do groups and institutions affect the behavior of individuals?

ROLE: *(You are ...)*
A public speaker

(Who is expected to ...)

COMPETENCE (Do what?)	CONTENT/CONCEPTS (With what?)	QUALITY CRITERIA ("Look fors")
Access and interpret by ... listing	the rules and required behaviors on your school	• Identify your purpose. • Brainstorm all possibilities. • Create two groups. • Clearly define the differences between necessary and unnecessary.
and categorizing	the rules you think are good, necessary for appropriate behavior, and those you think are unnecessary for maintaining appropriate behavior.	

COMPETENCE (In order to ...)	PRODUCT/PERFORMANCE (... do what?)	QUALITY CRITERIA ("Look fors")
Produce by ... developing	a chart showing the differences	• Review all possibilities. • Clearly depict the important ideas. • Select changes • Provide sound details.
and recommending	changes to the rules.	

COMPETENCE	AUDIENCE / SETTING (To/for whom? Where?)	QUALITY CRITERIA ("Look fors")
Disseminate by ... presenting	your chart and ideas to a group in your class	• Organize your approach and materials. • Speak to persuade. • Defend your position with details and examples.
and justifying	your recommendations as good for whole school.	

SAMPLE PERFORMANCE DESIGNER GRADE 8

PURPOSE:
To draw a conclusion

SOCIAL STUDIES:
CIVIC IDEALS AND PRACTICES
(SEE PAGE 74)

- -

KEY ORGANIZING QUESTION:
How can ordinary citizens influence policy decisions?

- -

ROLE: *(You are ...)*
A concerned citizen

(Who is expected to ...)

COMPETENCE *(Do what?)*	CONTENT/CONCEPTS *(With what?)*	QUALITY CRITERIA *("Look fors")*
Access and interpret by ... collecting and analyzing	information on an important local issue considered by your local governmental branch the development of this issue from introduction to decision or vote.	• Clearly state your purpose. • Identify possibilities. • Decide how and where to gather information. • Select information from a variety of resources. • Sequence the stages.

COMPETENCE *(In order to ...*	PRODUCT/PERFORMANCE *... do what?)*	QUALITY CRITERIA *("Look fors")*
Produce by ... designing and developing	a depiction of the process that includes your conclusions.	• Review the information. • Create a draft representation. • Include necessary details. • Edit for sequence and details. • Create the final form creatively.

COMPETENCE	AUDIENCE / SETTING *(To/for whom? Where?)*	QUALITY CRITERIA *("Look fors")*
Disseminate by ... presenting and distributing	your depiction to your classmates and to representatives from your local governmental branch.	• Organize your ideas. • Use standard conventions of public speaking. • Display the depiction. • Seek reactions.

SAMPLE PERFORMANCE DESIGNER FOR GRADE 12

PURPOSE:

To interpret for personal meaning

KEY ORGANIZING QUESTION:

What do popular terms mean when they are turned into action (for example, *equity, human dignity, rule of law, access*)?

ROLE: *(You are ...)*

A political investigator

(Who is expected to ...)

COMPETENCE (Do what?)	CONTENT/CONCEPTS (With what?)	QUALITY CRITERIA ("Look fors")
Access and interpret by ... collecting analyzing and deciding	information from a wide variety of resources on the use and meaning of the term *equity and access*, the collected data, what it means to you.	• Clearly state your purpose. • Decide how and where to gather information and evidence. • Compare and contrast the collected data. • Select the most pertinent data for your purpose.

COMPETENCE (In order to ...)	PRODUCT/PERFORMANCE ... do what?)	QUALITY CRITERIA ("Look fors")
Produce by ... designing and developing	a video script that displays your personal interpretation a video.	• Clearly define your intgended message. • Create a detailed storyboard. • Review and discuss alternatives. • Select your key ideas and pathway.

COMPETENCE	AUDIENCE / SETTING (To/for whom? Where?)	QUALITY CRITERIA ("Look fors")
Disseminate by ... broadcasting	over closed-circuit or cable television for your classmates and community members.	• Arrange details. • Expand to the fullest extent. • Create the video. • Identify the arrangements. • Contact the necessary people. • Broadcast the video. • Seek reactions and responses.

APPENDIX: BLANK TEMPLATES

PERFORMANCE DESIGNER

PURPOSE:

- -

KEY ORGANIZING QUESTION:

- -

ROLE: *(You are ...)*

(Who is expected to ...)

COMPETENCE *(Do what?)*	CONTENT/CONCEPTS *(With what?)*	QUALITY CRITERIA *("Look fors")*
Access and interpret by ...		

COMPETENCE *(In order to ...)*	PRODUCT/PERFORMANCE *... do what?)*	QUALITY CRITERIA *("Look fors")*
Produce by ...		

COMPETENCE	AUDIENCE / SETTING *(To/for whom? Where?)*	QUALITY CRITERIA *("Look fors")*
Disseminate by ...		

Burz and Marshall. *Performance-Based Curriculum for Social Studies: From Knowing to Showing.* © 1998 by Corwin Press, Inc.

Social Studies:
Grade ___

**Performance
Benchmark**

CONTENT/CONCEPT STANDARD ___

KEY ORGANIZING QUESTION:

KEY COMPETENCES	KEY CONCEPTS AND CONTENT	PERFORMANCE TASKS
		PERFORMANCE TASK I:
		PERFORMANCE TASK II:

QUALITY CRITERIA:

Burz and Marshall. *Performance-Based Curriculum for Social Studies: From Knowing to Showing.* © 1998 by Corwin Press, Inc.

Technology Connections
_____ : Grade ___

**Performance
Benchmark**

KEY ORGANIZING QUESTION:

ACCESS	PRODUCE	DISSEMINATE
PERFORMANCE TASK I:	**PERFORMANCE TASK I:**	**PERFORMANCE TASK I:**
PERFORMANCE TASK II:	**PERFORMANCE TASK II:**	**PERFORMANCE TASK II:**

BIBLIOGRAPHY

Albertman, L., & McMahon, E. (1985). *Street law: A course in practical law.* New York: Viking-Penguin.

Anderson, J. (1986). *The glorious fourth at Prairietown.* New York: William Morrow.

Appy, C., DiBacco, T., & Mason, L. (1991). *The history of the United States.* Boston: Houghton Mifflin.

Atwood, V. A. (Ed.). (1986). *Elementary school social studies: Research as a guide to practice.* Bulletin 79. Washington, DC: National Council for the Social Studies (NCSS).

Banks, J. A. (1984). *Teaching strategies for ethnic students* (3rd ed.). Boston: Allyn & Bacon.

Bishop, M. (1986). *Middle ages.* Lexington, MA: American Heritage.

Boehm, R. (1990). *Building skills in geography.* Urbana, IL: MacMillan/McGraw-Hill.

Boehm, R., & Swanson, J. (1992). *World geography* (3rd ed.). Columbia: Macmillan/McGraw-Hill.

Brown, B. C. J. (1993). *History and social science curriculum framework.* Manuscript in preparation. District of Columbia Public Schools.

Budin, H., & Kemdall, D. S. (Eds.). (1987, January). Computers in social studies. *Social Education, 51,* 32-59.

Clark, J. R., & Wilson, H. (1988). *Economics: The science of cost, benefit and choice.* Chicago: South Western.

Costa, A. L. (1985). *Developing minds: A resource book on teaching thinking.* Richmond, VA: Association for Supervision and Curriculum Development.

Coulon, J., & Krieger, L. (1990). *World history: Perspectives on the past.* Lexington, MA: D.C. Heath.

Crabtee, C., & Ravitch, D. (1988). *California state framework: History and social science.* Sacramento: California Department of Education.

Davis, J. E. (Ed.). (1983). *Planning a social studies program: Activities, guidelines and resources.* Boulder: Colorado Social Science Education Consortium.

Dobler, L. (1962). *Customs and holidays around the world.* New York: Fleet Press.

Engle, T. L., & Snellgrove, L. (1989). *Psychology: Its principles and applications.* Chicago: Harcourt Brace Jovanovich.

Flanagan, J. C. (1971). *Social studies behavioral objectives.* Palo Alto, CA: Westinghouse Learning Press.

Gardener. D. P., et al. (1983). *A nation at risk: The imperative for education reform.* Washington, DC: National Commission on Excellence in Education.

Gertz, B. (1983). *Understanding the law.* New York: McDougal, Littell and Co.

Greenblatt, M., & Wilty, P. (1992). *The human expression: World regions and cultures.* Columbus, OH: Macmillan/McGraw-Hill.

Hammack. D. C., et al. (1990). *The U.S. history report card: The achievement of fourth, eighth, and twelfth-grade students in 1988 and trends from 1986 to 1988 in the factual knowledge of high school juniors.* Princeton, NJ: National Assessment of Educational Progress, Educational Testing Service.

Helgren, D. M. (1985). *World geography today.* New York: Holt, Rinehart & Winston.

Jackson, K. T. (1988). *Building a history curriculum.* Bradley Commission on History in Schools. Washington, DC: Educational Excellence Network.

Jarolimek, J. (1985). *The United States and the other Americas.* New York: MacMillan.

Keller, S., & Lademan, L. (1994). *Who are we? Stories of migration and immigration.* Lexington, MA: D.C. Heath.

Krieger, L., & Peck, I. (1980). *Sociology: The search for social patterns.* New York: Scholastic.

Kurfman, D. (Ed.). (1977). *Developing decision-making skills.* 47th yearbook. Washington, DC: National Council for the Social Studies.

Leinwald, G. (1983). *The pageant of world history.* Boston: Allyn & Bacon.

Martelli, L. (1985). *Earth's regions.* New York: MacMillan.

Melder, K., et al. (1983). *City of magnificent intentions: A history of the District of Columbia.* Washington, DC: Associates for Renewal in Education.

Miller, R. (1991). *Economics: Today and tomorrow.* Mission Hill, CA: Glencoe/McGraw-Hill.

National Council for the Social Studies. (1994). *Curriculum standards for social studies: Expectations of excellence.* Bulletin 89. Washington, DC: Author.

Parker, W. C. (1991). *Renewing the social studies curriculum.* Alexandria, VA: Association for Supervision and Curriculum Development.

Pierce, N. R. (1983). *The book of America: Inside fifty states today.* New York: W.W. Norton.

Prolman, M. (1969). *The story of the constitution.* Chicago: Children's Press.

Remy, R. C. (1980). *Handbook of basic citizenship competencies.* Richmond, VA: Association for Supervision and Curriculum Development.

Resnick, A. (1983). *Russia: A history to 1917.* Chicago: Children's Press.

Sanders, P. (1980). *A framework for teaching the basic concepts* (2nd ed.) New York: Joint Council on Economic Education.

Sanders, P., et al. (1984). *Master curriculum guide in economics: A framework for teaching basic concepts* (2nd ed.). New York: Joint Council on Economic Education.

Schner, A., & Wallbank, W. (1987). *History and life: The world and its people.* Glenview, IL: Scott, Foresman.

Seefeldt, C. (1984). *Social studies for the preschool-primary child.* Columbus, OH: Charles E. Merlin.

Shuster, A. A. (1971). *Social science education in the elementary school.* Athens, OH: Charles E. Merlin.

Steeg, C. (1991). *Exploring regions—near and far.* Lexington, MA: D.C. Heath.

Stephano, M., & Leonard, J. L. (1993). *Southridge middle school history department program: California Demonstration School.* Sacramento, CA: State Department of Education.

Walter, P. (Ed.). (1987). *Social studies curriculum software reference guide. K-12.* Cupertino, CA: Apple Computer.

Welty, P. T. (1992). *The human expression—World regions and cultures.* Urbana, IL: Macmillan/McGraw-Hill.

Wolf, A., & Ellwood, R.. (1991). *Teaching about world religion: A teacher's supplement.* Boston: Houghton Mifflin.

Wrangham, E. (1980). *The communications revolution.* New York: Green Haven.

Zimolzak, C. E., & Stansfield, C. A. (1983). *The human landscape* (2nd ed.). New York: Charles E. Merlin.

CORWIN
PRESS

The Corwin Press logo — a raven striding across an open book — represents the happy union of courage and learning. We are a professional-level publisher of books and journals for K–12 educators, and we are committed to creating and providing resources that embody these qualities. Corwin's motto is "Success for All Learners."